Bill & Joan —
with, I hope, happy memories of
Naivasha, Kenya.
H.

"I'm Only the Editor"

The Adventurous Life of Journalist Charles Hayes

Margaret A. Hayes

The Adventurous Life of Journalist Charles Hayes

Margaret Ann Hayes

Trafford Publishers, Victoria, BC, Canada

Book Design by Margaret Hayes

Other books by Margaret Hayes:

Kenya Diary,
Kenya Litho 1976.

Where the Tarmac Ends; to East Africa with Love,
Rima Books 1989.

The South Okanagan Review Cook Book and Prose,
Rima Books 1992.

Printed in Victoria, Canada.

Note for Librarians: a cataloguing record for this book that includes Dewey Classification and US Library of Congress numbers is available from the National Library of Canada. The complete cataloguing record can be obtained from the National Library's online database at: www.nlc-bnc.ca/amicus/index-e.html

ISBN: 1-4120-1411-5

TRAFFORD

This book was published *on-demand* in cooperation with Trafford Publishing. On-demand publishing is a unique process and service of making a book available for retail sale to the public taking advantage of on-demand manufacturing and Internet marketing. **On-demand publishing** includes promotions, retail sales, manufacturing, order fulfilment, accounting and collecting royalties on behalf of the author.

Suite 6E, 2333 Government St., Victoria, B.C. V8T 4P4, CANADA

Phone	250-383-6864	Toll-free 1-888-232-4444 (Canada & US)
Fax	250-383-6804	E-mail sales@trafford.com
Web site www.trafford.com		TRAFFORD PUBLISHING IS A DIVISION OF TRAFFORD HOLDINGS, LTD.
Trafford Catalogue # 03-1789		www.trafford.com/robots/03-1789.html

10   9   8   7   6   5   4   3   2

A writer is a funny man,
So I have heard it said,
Unlike all other animals,
His tale grows from his head.

Anonymous

Foreword

Soldier, colonial administrator, linguist, actor, hotelier, environmentalist, broadcaster, editor and publisher, Charles Hayes was a Renaissance man of a type rarely seen in these more sedate times. In a volume which ranges from pre-World War II London through wartime Burma and India to the mesmerizing beauty of Kenya and finally to anchorage in British Columbia, Canada, Margaret Hayes chronicles an astonishing life with wifely tenderness and professional precision. Calling upon her own talents as a writer and reporter and making use of a jumble of files and a lifetime of memories, Mrs. Hayes has woven a magical tapestry.

Those who knew Charles Hayes will see him come alive again in these pages: those who did not know him will come as close to his impetuous, bright-eyed enthusiasms as this esoteric experience allows. Margaret Hayes has introduced us to a new literary genre: the love letter as biography. And what a billet-doux it is!

Gerry Loughran,
Retired Journalist

Preface

It took three months after the death of my husband, Charles Hayes, in April 2000, before I could bring myself to open the old journey-battered, four-drawer filing cabinet stored in our Canadian house since moving there from Kenya, East Africa in 1980. We had always meant to open and sort out the files together, but once we had started publishing our weekly newspaper, *The South Okanagan Review*, there never seemed time. Even in our busy office Charles would pass talkative visitors over to me, or to our daughters who worked with us, saying, with a charming smile, "Forgive me, but I'm only the editor, would you please talk to Margaret, or Jane, or Caroline as I'm working in seconds."

Reading his well-organised files, compiled so many years ago, became a quiet healing time as it drew me into my husband's captivating adventures from when he lived in England, in the 30's, to his time during WW2 as Major in The Queen's Own Cameron Highlanders, seeing action in Burma. His written documents gathered momentum when I read of his arrival in Simla, India, where he was present at the partition of India and Pakistan in 1946/7.

From India he travelled to Kenya and was instrumental in starting the first Kiswahili newspaper, finally becoming editorial director of the (Kenya) *Nation Group of English language newspapers* with the largest circulation in East Africa. As foreign news correspondent for the BBC, (British Broadcasting Corporation), I could see by his efficient filing system, a day-by-day history had evolved. The content of those files was like a book so full of interest that I couldn't put it aside. After reading his last entries, I decided that indeed a book had to be written.

Charles was an amazing, unforgettable man, a great writer, a precise editor and whatever the crisis, always a gentleman. Our chance meeting in 1964 became a lasting wonderment for us. He was my dearest love, my mentor and my best friend.

I'm Only the Editor is dedicated to our shared children, Christine, Michael, Jane, Julian, Roger, Judith and Caroline, their spouses and our 14 grand children. It would have given Charles great joy to know his two great-grandchildren, Conner and Samantha Rougier-Chapman, born after his death in the year 2000.

Margaret Ann Hayes
Okanagan Falls, British Columbia, Canada
2004

Table of Contents

Charles Hayes senior returns to England, having served with the Royal Horse Artillery in France, WW1, and is united with his wife Caroline Helena Hayes and his young son Charles. Croydon. 1918

ONE

The First Years

*"There's many a boy here today who looks on
War as all glory but, boys, it is all hell."*
Gen. William T. Sherman, Address (1880)

FROM THE MOMENT a chubby ten-pound baby boy slid, none too easily, into the world, his rich voice has made people stop in their tracks; women's eyes to glaze over. Even the doctor attending the birth raised a surprised eyebrow as this baby opened a wide mouth and crooned a soft, melodic herald to his early morning arrival.

This was not the usual screamer, hospital staff decided.

Charles Arthur Andrew Hayes was born in Croydon, England, on March 18th, 1915. His petite mother, Caroline Helena Hayes tried *so* hard to deliver her first child on Saint Patrick's Day, but Charles junior took his time arriving, as would be his fashion throughout life, (though often endearingly), ten minutes or more late.

That March his father, Charles Hayes, was in France with the Royal Horse Artillery, a part of the famous "E" Battery, which led horse-drawn carriages through cold, often mud-thick battlefields during the bloody fighting of World War I.

On August 14th, 1914, when war was declared between England and Germany, Charles Hayes senior, already a reservist with a Field Battery of Artillery in the South African Boer war, (1899 to 1901), went straightway to join his regiment in order to fight in France, leaving, sadly, his young pregnant wife.

During the following long, war-darkened years, when Germany's fat, silver zeppelins, filled with bombs, hovered like huge, shiny maggots way above the outskirts of London, and the horror of young soldiers being gassed and killed in overseas trenches was every day news, Caroline Hayes decided, as did one million young British women in order to help the war effort, to work in one of the many munitions factories which had started up in the outskirts of London.

The throng of dedicated women at a Woolwich Arsenal factory knew that packing explosives into heavy metal shell cases was dangerous work. Nevertheless, they carried on, often working overtime 'to get the show on the road,' they said. Sometimes women were blown up when something went wrong with the TNT explosives, and they knew that an exploding shell in a crowded factory would be a terrible experience. TNT poisoning was 'like the flu coming on', the women were advised, and those whose skin became yellow because of it were known as 'canaries'. Then there was the evil smell of acid particles hovering around the factory, but the women were hell-bent on Britain winning the war at all costs.

Young Charles remembered being held up to the window by his mother to watch zeppelins floating 'very slowly' across the sky towards the inner city of London.

"They looked so beautiful, gleaming in the evening sunlight, but I didn't realize, at the age of two, how dangerously full of bombs they were. One evening my mother and I watched a zeppelin burst into flames and come tumbling down into a park. It looked like a huge sausage losing it's burnt, flaming skin."

In 1918 Charles Hayes (senior), by then a disabled man, arrived home to Croydon in time for Christmas. The young Charles thought his father's arrival was a wondrous occasion when meeting his father for the first time.

"With a wide grin across his face my father picked me up and I remember, quite clearly, that he stared at me for a long, long time." The youngster soon learned that his father's lungs had been badly damaged by often-deadly mustard gas fumes that the enemy had blown

The young Charles Hayes at 6 years old. England, 1921.

through the trenches of France and Belgium in an effort to kill off the British and their allies. Charles also remembered, with more curiosity than concern at his young age, how his father's lungs would sometimes whistle when he became short of breath.

"Those are gas-burned holes in there, my son," his father would smile, blue eyes twinkling, although at the time he must have been in pain. He told us about 'trench warfare' when the green, then the mustard gas flowed through the trenches in the Battle of the Somme and how the British bombardment sent 100 thousand shells a day over the German dugouts until they crumbled. But the single worst day in English Military history, he said, was when 20,000 men of the 90th Brigade were killed, and with the smell of cordite hanging in the air, 40,000 wounded were rushed to tented makeshift field hospitals.

"My father went on to tell us about the tour of the battlefields by King George V, during which time it rained and rained and rained, with horses and soldiers drowning in huge, rain-filled shell holes. A yellow slime covered the thick mud patches and swamps which made it even more difficult to know where the deep holes were. My father's war stories have remained with me forever."

When Charles was about six years old he was taken to see his first silent black and white film. The local cinema was showing cowboy Tom Mix, and a shoot-out with Red Indians.

"I was so taken up with the film, and what hero Tom Mix was doing, that I ran to the piano at the front of the cinema shouting, "Look out Tom, he's right behind you!" The audience roared with laughter. My embarrassed mother dragged me back to my seat.

"Over the next few months I would show her that I was not a complete idiot, so learned the Welsh name of the second longest place name in the world. It had 58 letters so I kept writing it and saying it over and over. Once learned I never forgot it, but I must have bored everyone by my chanting, on every possible occasion, Llanfairpwllgwyngyllgogerychwyyndrobwllllantysiliogogogooch,   which translates as: 'Saint Mary's church by the white aspen over the whirlpool, and Saint Tysilio's by the red cave.' The whole wording fascinated me. The town is now officially known as, Lanfair, P.G."

Charles had a best friend, a big white duck he kept in the garden. After dinner one evening, his grandfather congratulated Charles' mother on the fine meal she had served.

"Oh, that was Charles' well- fed duck," she smiled.

Horrified, the young Charles ran to the bathroom where, through his tears, was violently sick. "I've eaten my friend, we are all cannibals," he cried. Inconsolable for days, he vowed never again would he eat a bird of any sort. And he didn't. Even in his old age he agreed that his loathing of eating chicken, turkey or duck, was mainly 'in his head', but still he couldn't eat any type of poultry.

"Could you eat your dog if it was your best friend?" was his reply when questioned. But eggs were never a problem. It was the only food he ever learnt to cook.

Over the next few years father Charles Hayes enjoyed the closeness and love of his wife and young son, regaling them with adventure stories and history. Thursday evenings was a time for talking about South Africa and eating fresh mussels cooked in a large pot on an open fire. Although the young boy thought that 'Africa-talk', coupled with mussel eating, was something of an enigma, the thrill of listening to African stories, always the main topic on those special evenings, was worth every minute of eating shellfish.

As a young man, Charles Hayes senior had lived in the country that became Southern Rhodesia and, like so many, he came under the influence of empire builder, Cecil Rhodes, of whom he spoke frequently with admiration. The family imagined they would all go to live in that splendid country one day.

The young Charles experienced many poignant moments, especially when his father took him walking to 'look at things'.

One Sunday he was shocked and very saddened when he saw his father cry. They were standing together in London's Hyde Park watching the dedication of the Royal Horse Artillery's famous monument, which showed soldiers and their horses dragging gun carriages through the mud of war-torn France. It was a carving on the face of a huge stone monument, a bas relief, describing the stories about which he had told so vividly; a devastating reminder for the young boy's father who had lost so many of his friends during those terrible war years.

One of the happier memories, Charles talked about, was when his father brewed what he called 'bee's wine'.

"On the flat surface of a stone slab, set into a shaded corner of our living room, stood a large earthenware crock filled with some honey-based concoction. A muslin cover, loaded down with coloured beads at its edges, was always in place over the frothy mixture, which from time to time, he invited me to inspect and to sample. My father gave me the nickname of 'the brewer', because I liked the honey mead so well."

On other occasions, when father and son attended meetings, CH senior would explain clearly what was going on and the history, always the history, of the event.

"In summertime my father would sometimes take us to Norbury, on the road that went north to London, where an old, well-known coaching house, with its beautiful, flowered garden, became a halfway rendezvous for members of our family."

The Hayes' family were staunch Irish Protestants, but to one religious meeting Caroline's father, Grandfather Charles Edward Wood, went along too.

"I was so embarrassed when Grandfather suddenly grabbed my hand and dragged me out of the meeting.

"'I schmell a papisht,' he growled in his deep Irish accent. 'We must leave.'

The Royal Horse Artillery monument, unveiled in Hyde Park, London. Shown below in *bas relief*, horses being dragged through the mud of France during WW1.

"Grandfather Wood would snort on about St. Patrick having cleared the snakes out of Ireland but, he would almost explode, 'he was made a saint for bringing Catholicism to the country!'"

Although brought up in the tradition of Protestant versus Catholic, the young Charles could never truly understand the hatred that differences of opinion over religion could instil. Although he would point out, in later years, that this sort of behavior should not surprise us.

"It's often not so much religious practices but political objectives, but there has been 'ethnic' cleansing in the world for as long as can be remembered. Just name a country and one invariably finds strife and warfare between people who have opposing religious beliefs."

Happier evenings were spent with music and dancing in the family household when Grandfather Wood, his wife Grandmother Matilda Jane (Crawford) and young Charles' parents would teach him to Irish 'step dance' on the large, stone-flagged kitchen floor.

"Keep yer arms down straight by yer side, me boy," insisted his adoring tutors as Grandfather, having opened a big wooden cupboard and chosen a musical instrument; sometimes a fiddle, or a woodwind, (he really enjoyed the piccolo), began to play, a master of them all.

Then the dancing would begin, sometimes lasting for hours, accompanied by much laughter and joy as the youngest, cosseted family member learnt his steps.

"Grandpa's Irish fiddle music made the house come alive, then, every now and again, with encouraging grunts he would nod towards me and to the family, saying, ' The boy's leppin' like a hare.'

"I was pleased to hear that!"

In 1924, as CH senior ran to catch a bus, he waved to Caroline, who stood at the garden gate, happy in her sixth month of pregnancy. Then, with shock, she saw him fall. Before she could reach him, her husband was dead. The years of strain on his heart, after wartime poisonous mustard gas had ruined his lungs and therefore his health, had taken its toll and he died instantly on the Croydon road two days before Christmas.

Nine-year-old Charles was sent to his Braidwood relatives for about three weeks while his father's funeral was organised and his mother rested. His cousin, John Braidwood, was 19 years old. At that time, the age difference was too great for them to become close friends. But fifty years later John Braidwood became an advisor and friend to Charles and was instrumental in Charles' move from Africa to Canada. John had moved there with his wife and two daughters, after WW2, to a small lakeside town named Naramata, in the Okanagan Valley, British Columbia. Having been held prisoner of war in a Japanese concentration camp for several years, John was very happy to settle in a new country. He built a large log house he named Sandy Beach Lodge, with outside swim pool, cabins, tennis courts and fruit trees edging along the shore of his Lake Okanagan property.

When Charles returned home from school one day, after that sad winter, he was delighted to find he had a baby brother named William Crawford who had been born on March 3rd, just 15 days before his 10th birthday. He learnt, from Grandpa Woods, that 'Bill' had been named after Prince William of Orange, a Protestant from Holland's Province of Orange. The Dutchman was invited by the opponents of King James II, (who had converted to Catholicism), to invade the country. William of Orange landed at Torbay, Devon in 1688 with an English and Dutch army, forcing James II, King of England and Ireland 1685-88, (known as James VII in Scotland), to flee.

In 1689, William (now William III) and his wife Mary II were proclaimed joint rulers. They came to the throne a year later.

Warming to the subject, Grandfather Wood continued, "William's decisive victory at the Battle of the Boyne, fought in Ireland near Drogheda, County Louth, between Protestant forces and the smaller Catholic forces led by James II, enabled him to capture Dublin, 'putting down' the Catholics and knocking nine bells out of 'em," chuckled Grandfather, rubbing his hands together with glee, "thus arriving at a critical stage in the English conquest of Ireland."

"King William couldn't speak the English language," grandfather Woods went on to explain to young Charles, "nevertheless the Irish adopted the King, inviting him to establish a Protestant monarchy.

"It was then that a group of men, naming themselves 'The Orangemen,' were set up in Ireland in order to carry out King William's wishes."

The anniversary is celebrated annually by Protestants, who march through Catholic areas in Northern Ireland on July 12th, known as 'Orangeman's Day'; the month of July as Ireland's 'Marching Season'.

William of Orange died childless in 1702, shortly after his wife Mary had passed away, but there was continuous rivalry between the Catholic Popes; one from Provence, France, and one from Rome; France providing their own Popes chosen at the '*Papes*' Palace in Avignon. They finally settled their differences 300 years later.

Charles' maternal grandmother, Matilda Jane Woods, was a great influence on his life, taking him with her when visiting friends in Celest Hill, Croydon, making sure he behaved well during tea times with such people as the editor of *The Times* and other 'genteel' people like clergymen and their wives, their hats often bobbing with false cherries and flowers.

"None of these people seemed to have children," said Charles, "and I was often bored, but some summer afternoons I would sit with Granny on her favourite large, flat stone in the churchyard in St James Road where, on hot days, a heavy yew tree was our shade. It was there she told me stories about Ireland and our relatives there -- especially about a cousin she called 'Bracket Jemmy' who, she said, was a man who could take a heavy wheelbarrow and lift it by the handles when it was full.

"Her stories, always interesting and amusing, were usually accompanied by the sounds of the organist and choir as they practiced in the nearby church. She was an excellent pianist herself and insisted that I take piano lessons, which I began to enjoy once she had found a teacher for me.

"A daughter of Fintona's town clerk, Granny Woods was well educated and her stories and teachings rubbed off on me. In retrospect, I realize that she got out of telling me her age by saying that the church records had been burnt! I think she distanced herself somewhat from her husband, Grandfather Woods, who was a political Orangeman -- a very astute militant. She was a more understanding Protestant, who went by the bible.

"As an evolutionist, Grandfather regarded bible teachings as fairy tales."

12 I'm Only The Editor

TWO

Irish Background

Religion is the opium of the people.
Karl Marx

CHARLES JUNIOR was 14 years old when he was on his way to Ireland for the first time and it was there that he learnt more about religious hatred.

On the ferryboat from Holyhead to Dublin, (Dun Laoghaire), the sea became very rough so he sat on the upper deck. Next to him, breathing in the salty air, was an old Irishman. Always ready to start up a conversation, Charles told the old man how his grandfather was a member of the Property Defense League (PDL) in Ireland, which was a civilian organization put together to defend Protestant-owned property. Charles, happy with the idea that he was actually related to a PDL member added proudly,

"They carry rifles, you know!"

The old man turned, and looking Charles straight in the eye said, "If I were you, sonny, I wouldn't mention that where you are going. They are all blackguards over there."

World War I had been over for seven years but there was much poverty and unrest in England, particularly in the northern counties. Charles recalled that in about 1926-7, when he was 12 years old, he watched crowds of people who had walked 250 miles, from Newcastle-on-Tyne to London, looking for work. There was no money to be earned in the shipyards or steelworks, so men, with their hungry and cold families, pulled carts and pushed prams filled with their goods and chattels.

"It was a very shocking sight."

He was a Boy Scout at that time and had been doing a lot of stage work - singing, dancing and acting - so when the Whitechapel area of London was also 'down on its knees', with little work for many, his 9th Croydon scout troop decided to give the poverty-stricken slum children a free 'Gang Show', a name then given to all Boy Scout shows everywhere.

That day the local Whitechapel cinema was filled with children who demanded an encore after Charles sang, (in his pre-teen falsetto voice), "When the Red, Red Robin goes Bob, Bob Bobbin' Along". He danced and walked with great confidence up and down the stage.

With whistling and hand clapping, shouting and foot stamping, the children went wild when Charles repeated his performance.

"I was so darned pleased with myself that I vowed I would become an all-time actor!"

The first Scout *Gang Show* was started just after WW I by Ralph Reader of Thornton Heath who also wrote the famous song 'The Gang's All Here; We're Sailing Along on the Crest of a Wave', first sung by 40 or more scouts during the original Gang Show held at the London Palladium. Over the following years the show was seen throughout England, Charles being a vigorous member on the stage in many towns, even playing the organ at one time when the musician didn't turn up.

"Simple stuff," said Charles, who had been taking piano lessons. "At least I sort of knew which notes to press," he laughed.

One such show took place at Wapping, somewhere at the back of the Thames, in a building later owned by Australian Rupert Murdoch, press king of the 1970's.

Charles, at this time, was attending John Ruskin's School in Croydon. Ruskin, an outspoken critic of the Arts in the late 1800's, was very much admired by Charles who insisted on being called 'Rusk' by his family. (Charles began calling his young brother Bill, 'Busk'). Up to the time of her death, his mother always began her letters to Charles, 'Dear Rusk'.[1]

In 1924, Charles won a John Ruskin essay competition, the first of many winning essays over the years, and was awarded a brown Ilford box camera presented to him at Croydon's Northend Hall by the editor of the *London Times*, Mr. Wickham Steed.

"The first picture I took with that camera was of a little girl. I had double exposed it so that it looked as if she was sitting on a wall, which she wasn't. I was quite pleased with that picture.

"Walking down High Street, after the award-giving ceremony, my mother took me to a well known café, maybe 'Fortes', where she ordered ice-cream and 'fancy cakes'. As I picked up the remaining crumbs with my fingers – they were too delicious to leave – my mother swatted me.

"'Don't you dare behave like that,' she said in a cross voice. My mother always watched my brother and me like a hawk at mealtimes, insisting that good manners were of absolute importance, chiding us quickly if we did anything wrong, especially at the table. Those lessons held us in good stead forever."

In the early 20's Grandfather Woods discovered a local business that had started recording sound on sixpenny silver disks, so, holding his grandson's hand, they marched together confidently into the store. Grandpa took his violin out of the case and started to play, which he did particularly well that day, Charles remembered. At the end of the recording session the silver disk was played back to the wide-eyed couple.

---

[1] A ferocious critic of capitalism and master of rolling English prose, John Ruskin was one of the great sages of Victorian England. The only child of a prosperous vintner from South London, Ruskin was born in 1819, publishing his first poem at age nine. Good looking, with bright blue eyes, he made his mark as art critic and social commentator. Eventually he went mad and died in 1900. (From John Batchelor's book, *Ruskin. Naked Truth.*)

"My dear chap, that sounds bad," said a deflated Grandfather. "Charles, sing something to cheer me up."

"All I could think of was 'Twinkle, Twinkle Little Star' and I was so nervous. We took those terrible disks home and kept them hidden in an old shoe box in the back of a dark cupboard under the stairs, the disks happily 'getting lost' over the years."

About that time, maybe 1927, Graves Ltd. of Sheffield produced crystal radio sets, which had a thin piece of wire called a 'whisker' attached to each, which had to be moved about carefully and sensitively in order to get good sound.

"I remember the day that Grandfather first heard the news on BBC, (British Broadcasting Corporation). He was so excited he had to get out a violin and play it. 'Dance boy dance, this is a historic moment', he laughed. And so we did."

During the 20's, Charles' uncle, Arthur Hayes, a sailor in the British navy, was headlined in *Reynold's Sporting News* as 'Champion Boxer of Britain's tough Mediterranean fleet'. As a contender in later world-title professional boxing bouts he was known throughout Britain and the European Continent as 'Champion Stopper Seaman Hayes'.

Since 1910, Arthur Hayes had excelled in boxing and, by the time his nephew was old enough to stand up, had taught Charles the correct moves to make a 'gentleman boxer'.

"No vicious stuff," his uncle Arthur insisted.

During the 1914-18 War he had been Britain's well-known featherweight boxer, so this well-experienced favourite uncle was persuaded to test out the youngster's 'attack mode'. Kneeling down, so that he was at Charles' height, (he was only 6 years old), uncle Arthur said, "punch me with your right and protect your face with your left."

Young Charles didn't protect his face, so got a punch on the nose for it.

"My uncle was almost in tears as he held me closely before taking me out for ice-cream. When I was a bit older he taught me well in the boxing ring telling me that a good boxer learns discipline, which keeps emotion and anger in control. Those lessons helped me stem any anger I felt on irritating occasions during my life."

By 1924, Arthur Hayes, with the wonderful wide smile and the memorable, soft-sounding voice, had top billing at London's Albert Hall where he was ready to fight 'French Tiger' Georges Carpentier. Young Charles had a ringside seat next to the great 'Bombadier' Billy Wells and watched as his uncle, who was being pummelled, leaned over the French Tiger's shoulder and, in a split second, with a confident smile, winked at his nephew.

"That's my uncle," thought Charles proudly.

Later, Arthur Hayes taught boxing at Eton College, England's prestigious public school for boys.

In 1927, Grandfather Woods was ill with pneumonia. Most days, during his illness, he lay in a bed set up beside a cosy stove. One evening, laying his violin beside him, he went to sleep more peacefully than he had done for some weeks.

Twelve-year-old Charles came running down stairs in the morning, always ready to greet his Grandfather, but found, instead, his mother binding her father's chin into position with a silk scarf. She had sat up all night with him while he dealt with his gradual death.

"I missed my grandfather very much. Although, when irritated, he could be a bit ferocious, he had in his head a wealth of knowledge. His stories and explanation of the things I wanted to know were all very real and exciting. Trained as a botanist at Trinity College, Dublin, he would come back from woodland walks, the deep pockets in his old tweed jacket laden with the things of nature he had found for me. Sometimes it would be a frog, which he plopped into a pond after showing me how it moved. Other pocket surprises were leaves, stones, flowers or insects, which he put under his microscope revealing a new world for me to think about.

"We all missed my father, and grandfather had done his best to make our loss less painful."

Seaman Uncle Arthur Hayes, champion boxer of Britain's tough Mediterranean Fleet, taught his young nephew, Charles, how to box.
(Pic. Reynolds Sporting News, 1924)

THREE

Childhood Memories

*"But the bravest are surely those who have the clearest
vision of what is before them, glory and danger alike
and yet, notwithstanding, go out and meet it".*
Thucydides

In May 1927, Charles was taken to Croydon aerodrome and was thrilled to watch Colonel Charles Augustus Lindbergh, United States aviator, touchdown after his memorable, non-stop transatlantic flight from New York to Paris.

Lindbergh had arrived from this amazing flight in his silver-winged plane, *Spirit of St. Louis.*

Twelve-year-old Charles remembered that the aviator looked exhausted, telling reporters in a tired voice that when he had arrived at Le Bourget Aerodrome in Paris, huge unexpected crowds of people surrounded him and his little plane. He was horrified to see, just minutes later, the sides of the airplane's fuselage full of gaping holes made by souvenir hunters who had even pulled a lubrication fitting off. Lindbergh saw his own helmet, perched on an American reporter's head, disappearing into the crowds.

After engineers at Le Bourget had repaired the aircraft Lindbergh took off for Belgium then went on to land at England's Croydon Aerodrome on May 29th where more thrilled and admiring crowds damaged a stabilizer. Repaired this time by Croydon engineers, the famous pilot flew on to nearby Gosport on May 31st where the *Spirit of St. Louis* was dismantled by the Royal Air Force, crated and placed onboard the US cruiser, Memphis, for its return voyage to the United States.[2]

In 1930, Charles became a member of the Croydon Histrionic Society. Critics came from all parts of the world to visit the high-powered Shakespeare Theatre Group. In one well attended play, fifteen-year-old Charles was chosen as a spear-carrier and was delighted to find himself on stage with actor Alex Guiness, (who was later knighted).

Another interest for Charles was to ride the non-stop Battersea to Purley 'atmospheric' railway that moved at tremendous speeds.

Charles said, "In 1840, after Stephenson's Rocket, the 'atmospheric' railway was much faster, with speeds up to 80 miles an hour. There was a piston inside a leather 'sleeve' which used to wear out so had to be replaced for every return journey. Driven by steam, the 'atmospheric' was superior to Stephenson's Rocket. My mother and I once found twelve feet of 'Rocket' rail in a grass-covered culvert near Croydon. In my teens the whole idea of that railway became of great interest to me and I couldn't read enough about it."

Another vivid memory Charles had of that year was when Gillett and Johnson, Croydon's church bell makers (carilloneurs) who made bells for customers all over the world, began making a full set of bells for a New Zealand church.

"For weeks the sound was adjusted by adding and subtracting metal parts so that the bells would sound perfect when completed. All day long, for weeks on end, the six-foot high bells sounded loud and clear all through the town and adjoining area. It was a most memorable time for everyone."

Charles also remembered, with great gusts of laughter, how he and his friends could never take their Saturday morning bible studies

---

[2] The official flight time of the *Spirit of St. Louis* from New York to Paris, on May 20th-21st, 1927, recorded by the National Aeronautic Association, was 33 hours, 30 minutes, 29 seconds. Lindbergh was the first pilot to achieve this record-breaking, *non-stop* transatlantic flight for which he was awarded $25,000 U.S.

seriously. He admitted that his schoolmaster, Mr. Robert Keelynack-Strick, discussed many aspects of the bible that interested them, but the whole morning study was coloured by a student named Tyndall who had a cunning knack of mastering the art of farting, turning each 'blow' into a high pitch as he squeezed his buttocks against the wooden bench on which he sat.

"His timing was superb," laughed Charles. "As some important piece of the bible was being discussed, so this thin, reedy sound would echo round the room and you never knew how long he would keep his special composition going. Every week poor, gentle old Strick would arrive looking apprehensive, then, when the inevitable 'squeak' started, Strick's eyebrows would shoot up and his eyes closed as if in pain. The squeak sometimes changed to a low growl, but Strick, hesitating for less than a heart beat, never made reference to the weekly 'incident', although our whole class shook with silent laughter."

Saturday afternoons in spring and summer Charles cycled with his friends to Carshalton Marshes, south of Croydon, to visit the cool, clear streams and catch newts, tadpoles and slimy, green-brown minnows which were taken home in old jam jars to study at leisure. Derby days would find him on Epsom Downs watching the huge buses and coaches filled with drunks who had attended the races. Children on sidewalks would shout at them, 'throw out yer mouldy' (meaning the copper coins that often looked green and mouldy); left-over change from race-goers' winnings.

In 1930, his last term at John Ruskin's school, Charles was chosen to fight an Irish student named Jimmy Twohig. As the evening drew nearer, Charles' mother said, "That boy will kill you. I'm coming along to the school."

Keeping his patience, Charles said slowly, "No Mum, mothers do not come to school boxing evenings." Nevertheless, she found herself a front seat. "I felt terrible," Charles said, "it was just a three-rounder and a very fair match. Jimmy eventually got to his feet. Then I saw my mother trying to clamber over the ropes. Defeated in her attempt, she then followed me to the dressing rooms telling everyone in her bubbly Irish way, 'that's my son, you know.' I just had to smile."

Later that night Charles went with his school friends to see their first colour film; a show featuring Al Johnson.

"A very thrilling end to school days," he decided.

FOUR

A New World

"Reading maketh a full man,
confidence a ready man
and writing an exact man".
Frances Bacon, '*Essays*'

BY THE TIME he was 18 years old Charles was studying to become a lawyer and enjoying London's city life.

Every morning he swam at the Croydon pool before running through Thornton Heath and Norbury to Streatham, Brixton, Newington Butts, where rifle practice went on, then past the Elephant and Castle pub to Southwick, and over London Bridge to Cheapside, where his office was located. "I ran so that I could save my train ticket money.

"There were so many wonderful things to do in the city. On hot summer evenings I would first swim in the Serpentine River then, all year round, I would go to boxing lessons. One evening a week I would change into my better dark suit and polished shoes for dancing at the Palladium with my friends. We partnered dance-perfect girls, who wore gorgeous long gowns, often entering ballroom dancing competitions.

"I remember, after one successful evening on the dance floor, we all celebrated with a bottle of cheap, sweet sherry. I was so sick afterwards that I never touched the stuff again.

"None of us seemed to sleep. Nights in the city were brilliant and wonderful with so much freedom."

London with its colourful lights, parties and hosts of new, modern-thinking friends, drew Charles more and more often into the city.

"Sir John Gielgud's sister worked in the same lawyer's office as I did, Wilberforce, Allan and Bryant, in Arundle Street in The Strand. Sir Ronald Wilberforce had gone on a cruise to Russia, which few people did in those days, and had met up with Gielgud's sister, subsequently offering her a job with his company. She was older than I but she took me to sophisticated Bloomsbury parties, introducing me to well-known actors. I became more smitten with the stage, but rather than become the lawyer my mother wanted me to be, I wanted to write.

"Sir Ronald used to wear 'tails'. He would lift them up and stand warming his bum against a gas fire when talking to us. We used to frequent Holly Lodge, Richard Thackerey's place in Hampstead, which was the Centre of Creativity. Thackerey started one of the great literarti magazines of the world – The Spectator."

Although by 1935 Charles was an articled clerk, writing was his first love so he bought himself a typewriter and quickly learned how to use it.

Due for his annual holiday, Charles booked a trip to Hungary where there was a worldwide Boy Scout Jamboree taking place at Estergom. Charles recalled that when he arrived at the Hungarian border, young, beautiful Hungarian girls gave a warm welcome and presented every passenger on the train a little basket of heart-shaped biscuits, each basket tied with fluttering ribbons.

"Nearing Munich, a German boy scout gave a Nazi salute, (which had just been brought in), as a return gesture to peasants who were planting their crops right up to the railway line. In his proud way, the boy had stuck his arm much too far out of the train window and his hand had been cut off immediately by a broken and bent iron pole that was leaning, crookedly, too near to the train. The train was stopped and the poor fellow was rushed to hospital leaving passengers in a state of shock."

Booking into the Gaillord Hotel, in Budapest, Charles enjoyed playing water polo in the famous pool there and watching, with amusement, grey-haired ladies giggling with pleasure each time a rush of water enveloped them from a new fangled 'wave machine', recently installed and obviously a great success. During this holiday Charles had time to relax and think carefully about his future.

On his return to London, Charles joined another firm of lawyers, George Bingham and Company, but again he felt he had had enough in the financial arena.

"I was becoming desperate to become a writer and it was such a draw with Fleet Street right beside me, so I visited all the old Cockney editors who kept telling me that when I learned shorthand I could apply for a job. There was the *Daily Mail*, *News of the World*, *Reynold's News*, *The Daily Express,* (housed in a modern building with a black marble façade), and *Reuters News Service* all beckoning me. I tried to learn the blasted shorthand, but never, ever conquered it."

Charles tried anything to get a foot into the world of news writing. He would pop into nearby city pubs at lunch time, getting to know reporters and eating such cheap but filling foods as sandwiches stuffed to the gunnels with potato salad and pickled eggs. Some lunch times were spent visiting his aunt Agnes, (one of four children born of his grandfather Hayes' second marriage), and her husband, Jack Milward, a quiet man who made the 'plates' (lithographs) for *Punch* magazine. At other times he would call on his Aunt Daisy, also from the second marriage, and her husband Gordon Garrett who had cornered the cheaper clothing market making wholesale garments for such large companies as Marks and Spencer's.

"It was fascinating to watch huge electric knives cutting through three-foot thick cloth laid out on wide cutting tables. Chalk lines, to form the patterns, were followed carefully but quickly. 'One mistake could easily cost you your life, or at least your hand, ' warned my uncle to his staff."

Charles was becoming bored with his work in a law office, so found himself a job as copy writer for Benson's Advertising, in Charing

Cross. This lasted a short time while he was still looking for a post with a newspaper.

He also began to see London with 'new eyes', especially after browsing old books found in city bookshops. "Living in London in the 30's and finding old, well-written books, opened up a world full of history and interest for me." He realized that a family's neighbours are important for children growing up together, often having an influence on each other.

As an ancient city port, Charles learned, London was, in the mid to late 1800's, unique. While it absorbed foreigners, it developed its own inner language, for instance the Cockney language, if you were born within the sound of Bow Bells; and there was a special pride in being one of an exclusive group, like the Pearly Kings and Queens. The crowded 'East End', on the fringe of the all-important City, had its own traditions. Shoreditch and Hoxton (or Hogstown), were geographic and economic descriptions of two specialized London areas – the conditions of the time being described vividly by Charles Dickens. Much of London's population then was poor and living by its wits.

There were few social amenities and people like Joseph Lister and Florence Nightingale had only recently introduced ideas like 'hygiene' into hospitals.

Nearing the 1900's, Islington, Charles read, was still in the countryside, a place where richer Londoners were seen on excursions to The Angel, a sophisticated meeting place for London's 'toffs' and the demimondaine underworld. On the way to Islington were poor houses, a hospital, a 'mad house' and its horrors, and prisons were still spewing out inmates who were being sent into exile from nearby Wapping Warf to colonize Australia.

In mid 1939, at 24 years old, Charles decided he needed to see more of the world so with a friend, Peter Hart from Nottingham, they travelled to Heidelberg, Germany. Charles avoided France, he said, because when he was 15 years old a pimp had tried to pick him up in Paris, which made him 'very angry'.

During their stay in Germany, Charles and his friend Peter spent several evenings with a group of German soldiers who they had met in a pub, The Rotenochsen, (The Red Bull), which had a pleasant, open air, top-of-the-town beer garden.

"A few of the soldiers invited us to the barracks at Mannheim, where we watched cadets training – just normal stuff. It was as relaxed as it could possibly be, but I did see work units carrying shovels on their shoulders, like one would a gun. At the time I thought it was a damned good idea that German youths were working on the projects that Hitler wanted.

"Since 1933 I had been watching, with interest, the rise of Hitler since he had become the Chancellor of Germany. Everywhere during that holiday, we saw the Hitler salute that I found came from the Roman way of greeting – the upward outstretched arm and hand. I thought at the time it was a wonderful thing to see, because in those early days Hitler was doing a lot of good things for the Germans, getting them off their knees and working hard with strict discipline to get them 'back on track', while England, in the early 30's, was in the doldrums."

Charles arrived back in England to read the *Daily Express* newspaper headline, 'There will be no war', while every other newspaper declared that war with Germany was imminent.

"I was completely shocked when, on Sunday, September 3rd, just a few weeks after arriving home from Germany, England's Prime Minister, Neville Chamberlain, announced that from 11 a.m. that day, England was at war with Germany.

"I kept denying it, saying that the Germans were not prepared for war. The songs we sang so recently with the young German soldiers in the pub and in their barracks held no hint of war. The ordinary

German people showed neither hatred nor any indication that within a month or so we would be enemies."

In England that September there was already much publicity on preparing for War. Still in shock, Charles watched ARP (Air Raid Precaution) duties being detailed. School children were each given a gas mask tucked into a square, brown, cardboard carrying-box complete with a long string for hoisting it onto their shoulders.

"The whole situation was unreal and frustrating. Television was just starting and I was on the fringe of becoming a writer."

At the first opportunity Charles set off for Grantham, where he had just joined the firm Tootal Broadhurst Lee, writing advertising copy for the Tootal range of Coutauld's Macclesfield Silks used in the making of their famous ties and scarves. He had toured their mills to see how the silk materials were spun and dyed.

"It was an in-between job before, hopefully, getting into newspapers."

Nevertheless, job or no job, Charles drove immediately to the nearest recruiting office where he wanted to enlist in the Irish Guards. By Sunday afternoon young men all through the country, knowing that Britain's freedom was at stake, were queueing up to join the Forces.

"Many of my friends were already 'Saturday soldiers', which had had no appeal for me, but when the blast of War sounded, I was in the queue. The trouble was that no one was really organised, because everything was happening so quickly. But finally a sergeant yelled out for us to leave our names and addresses and 'they would get in touch soonest'. This we did, and by the following week the manager for Tootals – a retired army major – was called up. I rang his house and asked his wife when he was going abroad.

"'Don't say that on the telephone', she whispered. 'Walls have ears you know'. And so the feeling of war-time secrecy started."

Charles kept working at his new job, waiting agonizing weeks to be 'called up'. To keep himself sane, he said, he attended musical concerts in Leicestershire, remembering clearly how large was the pianist, Constant Lambert and how 'thin', in comparison, was the piano he played so beautifully for the Covent Garden Ballet Company.

"As the dancers whirled and pirouetted, so clouds of dust flew out of the stage floorboards. I felt guilty watching ballet and musical concerts on my spare evenings, but army registration offices were not fully manned and just not ready to accept those who wanted to join the Forces. People were posturing, not really believing that such a huge event as War was about to happen.

"During the waiting game young men and women were getting married, wanting a partner, a symbol almost, of someone to fight for and, if necessary, someone to leave ones' belongings to.

"My girlfriend at that time was from an Irish Catholic family. My family, being Irish Protestants, made for difficulties.

"Beatrice May Josephine Venables and I didn't know each other well, but marriage everywhere was being encouraged 'for King, Country and Family'.

"Petrol rationing had just started and the rare times I came back to Croydon, (from Leicester), Beatrice's mother, Mrs. (Annie) Venables, and her husband kept insisting that their daughter and I married. One weekend there was a Priest in their house in Selhurst, north of Croydon, and suddenly I was being quizzed about my beliefs. Mrs. Venables said, 'Don't worry, it doesn't matter what you think about your religious beliefs as long as you marry in a Catholic church.' The reassuring thing was that it 'didn't matter,' as long as he said the right things to the Priest, such as that he believed in Almighty God and all that.

"I told Mrs. V. that frankly, through my upbringing as a Protestant, and with a grandfather who was an agnostic, I thought the whole procedure false and why couldn't Beaty and I just get married in a Registry office?"

Mrs. V said that a registry office wedding would not be acceptable.

"Then there was the tricky business of telling my fiercely Irish Protestant mother. As we neared the marriage date of December 1939, my mother said, almost in tears, that she couldn't possibly come to my wedding in a Catholic church, which made me realize how much I had offended her.

"I still thought she would come to the ceremony, but she told me later that she had stood at the back of the church to witness the marriage then, quietly and very sadly, went back home. It was a stupid, unhappy situation caused in the name of opposing religions."

Dropping the name Beatrice, (or Beaty, as some people knew her), Josephine and Charles boarded a train to honeymoon in Brighton, on the English coast.

"Had the army accepted me when I first registered, we probably wouldn't have got married at all then."

Charles Hayes marries Josephine (Beaty) Venables on December 23, 1939.

Within a few months Charles was selected for OCTU, (Officer Cadet Training Unit) in Wales, where he trained vigorously, running up and down mountain-sides and for miles in full equipment. From Wales he was sent to Inverness, Scotland, the base for The Queen's Own Cameron Highlanders.

"Although Britain had a King, it was still Queen Victoria's old regiment formed in her honour," Charles explained.

"The only outfitters commissioned to make The Queen's Own Cameron Highlander's uniforms were Robertson's of Princes Street, Edinburgh, who would send tailors to OCTU to measure-up uniforms for officers. Kilt hems, new officers learnt, must measure one inch from the floor when kneeling down. A khaki jacket, made of tough serge, is worn over a khaki shirt and a Cameron tartan tie. Khaki puttees, which start at the boot instep, are wound round and round up the leg to under the knee. Mostly for War, a battledress top and kilt is worn with a 'Sam Brown' leather belt with a crossed strap across the body. Always the Cameron emblem and rank are shown on both epaulettes.

"When I first arrived, dressed in my new uniform, to go into the officer's Mess, I saw a bear's rug, head and all, crawling across the room and growling at me."

The voice said, "I'm a bear, I'm a bear". Charles said to this drunk, "You're a bloody idiot." At that the bear stood up and said, "I'm your Colonel, sir." Red–faced, Charles introduced himself. His colonel said quietly, "Come and have a drink." The huge Mess room had a leather-topped, round-the-fire balustrade on which they sat to talk.

"Then came the conditioning," said Charles. "Because I was the youngest subaltern 'on the block', as it were, I was taken under the wing of the Regimental Sergeant Major, a wonderful older man who taught me the Highland Fling and the Scottish Sword Dance –which came directly from Scotland's heroic past war-torn years while pipes and drums have been synonymous with the small but celebrated nation for centuries – not so very different from the Irish dancing I had learnt as a child accompanied by my grandfather's fiddle music. But all dance lessons stopped for me for a while after I had an accident while riding my BSA 350cc motorbike. Driving round a curve too fast I smacked into a car, messing up my leg for some time, but as soon as I was able, it was back to Scottish dancing again. But there was little respite.

"Before reporting for parade each morning, we had to stand, feet astride, above a mirrored panel on the floor, presumably for the instructors to see if we were dressed properly, i.e. that we were not wearing underpants, as in true Scottish kilt-wearers' tradition.

"I had to be on parade in my kilt very early in the mornings until becoming dance proficient. In his broad Scottish accent, rolling his R's well, my sergeant said, day after day, 'Yer lazy Mr. Hayes Sirrr, pick up yer feet, Sirrrr.'"

This treatment went on and on, every early morning, until Charles passed his dance lessons.

"By mid-'41, just as Josephine had told me that we were expecting a baby, there was a sudden drafting for Singapore. The Japanese were on the move and the Norfolk Regiment was sent to fight. They went down with the ship.

"Pretty soon we were on one of those long journeys to escape the U-boats. There was a bunch of ENSA (Entertainments National Service Association) professional singers and dancers who were sent abroad to entertain the troops. I remember that they were very much in demand on a journey like this. I was leaning over the ship's rail one night, talking to an old west coast character named Palmy Pomeroy, a malaria controller in Nigeria. We were watching the phosphorescent lights in the tropical waters when he said, 'there's a phenomenon; light without heat.' Then he turned to the corridor behind us where the ENSA girls were and went on, 'there's another phenomenon; heat without light'. Smiling, he went back to watching the water.

Charles Hayes joins the Queen's Own Cameron Highlanders, 1940.

"We were sent into Ghana, West Africa, which suited me. I was, at the time, Platoon Commander, The Queen's Own Cameron Highlanders, seconded to the Gold Coast Regiment, part of the Royal West African Frontier Force. The Eighth Battalion of the Gold Coast Regiment, made up of the Nigerian, Gold Coast, Sierra Leone and the Gambia Regiments, was hastily thrown together. We wore on the left shoulder of our battle dress the Divisional emblem: a tarantula spider, black on yellow, the significance being, like that of the tarantula, once we had conquered we would never let go.

"To be sent to the northern most station of Kintampo, north of Kumasi, interested me very much as Lord Baden Powell, who started the World Boy Scout Movement, was there in 1897 or thereabouts. He had been drafted in from India to deal with the Ashanti Rebellion. BP learnt the left-handed handshake from the Ashanti tribe, using it ever more for the Boy Scout movement, which he started on Brown Sea Island on London's River Thames.

"It was about that time I was happy to hear that my wife, Josephine, had given birth to our daughter, Christine, on May 18th 1942 in Willisley Castle, Matlock, Derbyshire. I wondered how long it would be before I would see our first born. [3]

"There were no black officers in our regiment until 1942 when the first Sandhurst-trained African, 2nd Lieutenant Seth Anthony, (of the Ashanti tribe), arrived to join us. He was a very brave man who went on to win an MC in Burma. After Independence, Seth Anthony became a Major and was later made the Consul in Washington, D.C., becoming a very fine diplomat indeed."

---

[3] Willisley Castle had been taken over by England's Salvation Army for British officer's wives who were waiting to give birth. Over 4,000 babies were born there during WW II.

Crossing the Arakan River.

An inspection by the Commander of Allied forces, General Sir Oliver Leese of Monsoon Company, West African Frontier Force, on the Arakan River, 1943.
(West African photo service. Acra)

The Queen's Own Cameron Highlanders on the march to Kintampo.

To prepare for operations in Burma, the training of the Division -- three Brigades to a Division, three Battalions to a Brigade -- was conducted in Ghana's swampy, mosquito-ridden areas in similar humid conditions the troops would soon encounter.

"However," said Charles, "it is a misnomer that Africans know all about thick jungle. We had to teach and train them to move quietly and we had to learn the *Hausa* language with which to carry out our instructions.

"Eventually we arrived in Abeokuta, a horrible, snake-ridden area where an old Ashanti woman, the local witch doctor, came to cut a small 1-inch cross on the left cheek of all my African troops. It was to keep them safe in battle, she said. (And indeed, we didn't have a lot of casualties). I was told by the old woman, as she blew a fine white dust into my face, that I would never be in any danger from a snake."

Charles remembered, grimly, that shortly afterwards, while creeping through dense jungle at dusk, a large snake, dangling from a tree, fell into his face before dropping to the ground and slithering away in the opposite direction. Thinking it was a loose branch he had brushed it to one side.

Since that traumatic experience, Charles has walked through snake-infested swamps, eaten snake steaks in the western Indian Rockies, where his Muslim cook fried pieces of a 3-foot rattler, (headless, he noted, somewhat relieved), and was never bothered by snakes during his time in West Africa, India, nor East Africa, where he spent many years after the war.

"The white powder seemed to have worked," smiled Charles.

The Eighth battalion then marched the one hundred and thirty miles to Kumasi, crossing the Volta River to Kintampo.

"While marching along the river bank we heard a scream, followed by a lot of shouting. Earlier on we had seen a young girl filling a bucket from the river edge. Hearing the commotion, some of our troops rushed back to find villagers terrorized. The young girl had disappeared into the jaws of a crocodile. Both child and croc had vanished beneath the river's green and turbid waters. Only her little red bucket remained on the bank.

"Before that incident we were all ready to get a good wash in that river, but we decided to hold on and complete our march through the jungle where, with great relief, we found water.

"Gratefully we tore off all our filthy clothes and bathed in slow-moving rain forest rivers and 'still' ponds, with me standing out as the only white man amongst them, causing a few wide grins on the faces of my troops.

"Many of our men were knocked out with Bilharzia caught in the sluggish waters or ponds. There was also a lot of malaria in this area, but we were all very careful about taking our prescribed mepacrine tablets which kept us free of the fever but made our eyeballs turn yellow. And, of course, there was always the fear of contracting Sleeping Sickness, brought about by the bite of Tsetse flies, where infected people could be seen with their eyes wide open although fast asleep, and Black Water Fever -- a stage beyond malaria -- to contend with.[4]

"After our training," Charles continued, "we were put on board ship at Lagos from where it became a long trip around The Cape to India.

---

[4] Bilharzia;(schistosomiasis), is a debilitating disease caused by a parasite that can get into the circulatory system of man once it has passed through the skin. It enters the venous system of a person who stands or swims for any length of time in slow-moving waters or stagnant ponds. Ambling underwater snails, which live and breed in these stagnant waters, are the intermediary hosts. The hatching of the eggs in still waters is due to osmotic pressure. Eventually Bilharzia effects liver and bladder and once a person has been infected, urinating in this type of water can start the whole cycle again. Originally Bilharzia was found in Egypt by doctor-explorer Bilharz in 1852 and subsequently, (seven years later), it was found by S. Cobbald in a Mangebay monkey in the London Zoo. Reference, *Tropical Diseases*, by Sir Phillip Manson-Bahr.

Charles bathes with his troops in a rain forest river.

"We landed in Bombay about September 1943, just as the Monsoons were drawing to a close, entering the city through beautiful archways. We admired the Taj Mahal Hotel and the famous Yacht Club but right beside the outside walls of these beautiful buildings people were starving and begging on the streets. With all the riches and culture we realized India was still an impoverished country.

"Only too soon we were whisked off to finish training in a nearby jungle area and our Division, which was slated for a move down the Kaladan Valley, was assembled in the township of Dohanzari, in the Arakhan, Burma."

The first task there was to cut a jeep road for which Charles, as platoon commander, was in charge. In one month the West Africans had built a track that ran seventy-five miles through the most difficult country to debouch at Daletme, on the Kaladan River.

"Our next task was to build airstrips along the river bank. Africans, adept at bush clearing, completed the work with great rapidity.

"A month later we met the Japanese when, in an opening engagement, we overran an enemy post. Thereafter, meeting stubborn resistance from small detachments, we began pushing steadily down the Valley to Paletwa and Kyauktaw.

"Fighting-patrols of the Reconnaissance Regiment of the 81st West African Division then went on to conduct raids behind enemy lines. The intelligence gathered was crucial.

"Then, sometime in April, the Japanese counter attacked and our West Africans were caught by surprise, proving not so steady in defense as dashing in attack. Thrown into confusion, we were forced back again to the northwest of Kyauktaw, via pack-and-porter basis, to the Kalapanzin river on the flank of the main battle, while a detachment retired slowly up the Kaladan river covering the transport.

" At that point it was still touch and go whether or not Hitler would win the war."

FIVE

Into War

"We have enough religion to make us hate, but
not enough to make us love one another."
Jonathan Swift

CONTACT WAS MADE YET AGAIN with the enemy by the Sierra Leone Regiment who was able to get into some Japanese positions to bomb the enemy mortars, which had been giving a bit of trouble.

"We were coming under a lot of mortar fire from an 81mm fieldpiece, which had a very flat trajectory, and two of my men were killed," said Charles.

"As West Africans do not like to have anything to do with death, unless it is in the family, I ended up digging the graves myself. The men stood silently in shock; the death of their two troopers being a bad omen for them, they said.

"You couldn't move very far without coming under observation and my men were hit while standing at the very edge of the jungle.

"I wrapped their bodies in blankets, placed them into graves and, after a short prayer, covered them with earth and stones. There was no way we could get their bodies back to any sort of base as it was a very fluid situation. At times we didn't know where 'base' was, or where the other battalion was located. You were on your own and used your initiative.

"But the West Africans were very courageous. We had to cross a river at night in single file, rifles held high above our heads, with crocodiles all around us. We could feel the water vibrating, which was a very frightening experience. Suddenly the expected happened and the

41

second man ahead of me yelled as he was dragged under water. The African behind him just smashed his rifle over and over the croc's head until the reptile let go. We were all more than relieved to reach the riverbank without further incident. The African, who had been attacked by the croc, had bad gashes on his legs but he recovered well. I never did get to appreciate crocodiles."

At one point the Japanese had the divisional HQ surrounded on all sides. "They were very mobile and had infiltrated around us and we didn't even know it. Non-combatant troops had to take up weapons and repel the very stoic and brave Japanese. We took one prisoner who, three days before, had had his right arm blown off by one of our mortar shells. He was still fighting to avoid being taken prisoner. The equivalent of a Lance Corporal, his section of ten men had been instructed to attack and annihilate our Brigade.

"On the other side of the Kaladan River there were East African troops who had given us reports that the Japanese were coming up the road in buses to the Golden Pagoda, which we could see just across the river in Kyauktaw. We could hardly credit a 'bus trip' as being an accurate account. However, unbelievably, there they were and our East African troops had to jump into the crocodile-infested river and swim across to us. (Luckily the crocs had moved downstream).

"The fabulous Golden Pagoda was a beautiful sight and we were rather upset that Canadian Vengeance planes were dive bombing it in order to wreck it, although we realized, only too well, that hostile Japanese gentlemen were camped all round it and were probably using it for storage purposes. I remember it was a very lovely day with a clear blue sky when we watched these aircraft doing their stuff."[5]

---

[5] Parts of the Kaladan report were from Charles Hayes in an interview with A.F. (Tony) Day. CM CD. Canadian Air Force, for his book "The Air War over the Arakan."

Late 1944, then Captain Charles Hayes, number 186279, was shot in the leg and was evacuated to a casualty station where he contracted jaundice, remembering later that he had spent some time in a tent before being moved to Chittagong for an operation at the Military hospital there.

"They wanted to lop off my leg, but I absolutely refused to have it removed. Hospital staff were surprised that I actually healed, (I was not surprised). Some time later I ended up at a Medical Board in Poona where they wanted to send me back to England as unfit, but I got as far as the Reinforcement Camp after asking them to send me back to my unit at Dohanzari.

"While my leg was recovering, I used to walk from the hospital to the Ashram -– place of peace, a community where I looked through the vertical bars of huge locked gates to watch Mohandas Karamshan Mahatma Gandhi move to a podium where he held court.

"There was plenty of activity in the Ashram where he told the mostly white women and a few Indian women , 'In this place there is no work beneath us'.

"Gandhi's disciples cooked food and settled down to weave their cotton cloth and listen to him whose philosophy on peace was spreading round the world. He was heard to have said, "If people cannot get on together, then separate them." [6]

By the time Charles returned to his base, much had changed. In the mean time he had been promoted to major, the enemy was on the

---

[6] Charles, remembering back to 1931 when he was just starting out in the law offices in England, noticed how Londoners had laughed at Gandhi when, in cold February weather, he arrived wearing only a hand-woven cotton *dhoti* (loin cloth) and *shuka* (sheet). He had been invited by British Government to attend London's Round Table Conference on Indian Constitutional Reform. Ghandi, who said, "Christ showed us the way, I will show you the method," was previously leader in the passive resistance campaigns that had begun in South Africa in the 1920's.

run, war in the Arakan had almost ended and soon all troops were to be pulled out and sent to Madras.

In 1945, Major Charles Hayes was offered a Brigade appointment as D.A.A.G. (Deputy Assistant Adjutant General) in Madras, where he was given a special assignment with AFI (Auxiliary Forces India) to de-mobilise troops at Fort Madras.

"I lived in the Duke of Wellington's rooms with all the East Indian books dating back to the time India had opened up for Queen Victoria.

"It was a very interesting time for me to study the history of that era. I was left in Madras as the sole representative for the two West African Divisions with my own Headquarters, the West African Liaison Service, dealing with the Government of India to clear out all West African troops and get them onto ships to go home.

"Congress Party leader Jawaharial Nehru, known as Pandit (teacher), who had been educated at Britain's Harrow and Cambridge and had become a lawyer, gave orders that no African must remain in India, so I had to track down many of my troops, sometimes tearing them from the bosoms of their new Indian families.

"Indian women loved the large West Africans with their rippling muscles, believing them to be black Gods, part of the Hindu Pantheon; the Deities.

"When I had found them all, which took a long and frustrating time, we decided, together, to give a farewell concert. There were many weeks, we felt sure, in which to organize a Show as the ship to take them back home would be a long time arriving.

"My Colonel had set up a hundred acres for two Divisions for African troops and their camps. One part was called 'The Garden of Eden'; a brothel for the West Africans, which certainly kept them from straying away again. On this acreage was also a most wonderful natural stage in a sort of outside Hollywood Bowl. I was in charge of theatre and, for some time, the stage became a place for African musicians and comedians to put on their own shows. The dancers wiggled their arses and the 'funny men' kept everyone laughing. West Africans are natural actors, singers and dancers and have a wonderful sense of humour. They stuffed pillows into their trousers to give themselves huge stomachs, made enormous shoes for their already big dancing feet, and there were passionate drummers. I wrote a rousing song for the last show with words that the 100–strong enthusiastic choir said they liked, and on the many days we practiced for the great last show, they sang it with tremendous gusto.

"On The Big Night I was sitting in the front row with the other officers. 3,000 excited Africans sat all round us, waiting. The show was going according to plan then, to my amazement the choir, which was to sing my 'rousing song', had changed tactics, singing their own song! The switch of my words made me laugh. They had beaten me. Africa had won again and the choir sang thrillingly, their blend of voices and harmony making it a memorable last night.

"They had spent much of their accumulated pay packets on visiting a Chinese dentist who had enrobed their front teeth with gold, as they said ' to impress our families back home.' The glitter of their wide smiles made for a happy time for most of them while they awaited their ship."

Charles attended the Madras Association meeting expecting that there would be questions from British Parliament about the West Africans and their escape, (for a while), into Indian families, but luckily nothing was mentioned about them.

"I became a member of the Madras Sculling Club, competing in sculling competitions on the Adyar River. I never did come in first though," said Charles dryly, but in the Madras newspaper it was reported that 'Major Hayes and Major Hamble, coxed by Major Horwood in the first heat, put up a good show against a far more experienced crew.

" For me," said Charles, " the sculling competitions were not as important as the religious building there, a Theosophical Centre, built on the river bank, which had been started by an American woman who had a Russian mentor. Can't remember their names, but I spent much time on that river on my own, which gave me time to think in those superb, peaceful surroundings.

"I needed that quiet time because I was due for six week's home leave and as I hadn't heard from my wife for many months, decided to go to England to look for her and our daughter Christine.

"I first travelled to Karachi then went by ship to Palestine then on to Jerusalem and Bethlehem, at that time a British Protectorate."

Headquarters Company 51st Brigade, 81st W.A. Frontier Division after the Burma engagement ended. 1945. (Major Charles Hayes center bottom row).

SIX

A New Start

"Comment is free, but facts are sacred."
C.P.Scott

WHEN CHARLES ARRIVED IN ENGLAND, he first bought an Armstrong Siddley car .

"Then I set about the search, finding, at last, a telephone number where my family might be. Josephine had moved about all over England, especially enjoying Guildford, where the Canadian troops were stationed.

"When I entered the house in Chesterfield, where they were then living, little Christine, just over 4 years old, stood staring at me. She had no smile, just looked at me inquisitively. It was very difficult for both of us as it was the first time we had seen each other. This little child who had been born during the war was breaking my heart.

"I learnt that Christine had been in hospital for three months after finding a bottle of nitric acid she had dug up in the garden. The bottle had broken, the contents spilling down her leg causing very deep blisters.

"Because Josephine and myself had had no contact for so long, our marriage was floundering. We talked about the three of us going back to India together, to finish off the months I would be stationed there. Josephine agreed that we should perhaps try to put our marriage together again, so I started negotiating with the War Office to get them a ship's passage as soon as possible after returning to my duties." [7]

Charles travelled back to India, his ship docking at Bombay at the end of December 1946. But once back in Madras, the first thing he had to deal with was to conduct a court marshal.

"The Sierra Leone boys, tired of waiting for their ship home, had entered the Armoury. When found out, they had started both a fire and a riot. So, as Judge -- appointed Deputy Assistant Adjutant General, a Brigade appointment -- I gradually listened to them all, recording evidence. Many of the guns taken from the armoury could not be found, so were probably thrown down wells during the strikers' panic. Some of the leaders were given prison sentences to start once they were back in West Africa which, shortly afterwards, they were.

"Josephine and Christine arrived by ship in January 1947. Once aboard a train it was a long and tiring three-day journey across India to my headquarters in Madras.

"We took over a large and airy Madras-style house with big marble pillars and hired an ayah (nursemaid) for Christine. I kept my

---

[7] Excerpts from a letter, (printed here), was sent many years later to his daughter, Christine, in which he summed up some of his thoughts and the sadness he had previously hidden:

"I remember the first time I saw you, in Chesterfield, you, looking beautiful and cool, nonchalant, busily solemn and eyeing me from time to time. Me, a little bewildered by the encounter with a four-year-old of whom I'd not even seen a picture, and by 1946 hardened (in perhaps the wrong ways, but war does that) from the man Hayes who had married your mother. Later, after we had gone to India, there were those infrequent visits to your hill school, in Simla, and prickly little family disagreements getting in the way and confusing all my hopes; the move to Kenya and the blinkered attempt to begin to build our foundations, and the failure. Then, lonely in the Rift Valley, (Nakuru) watching what I thought to be your 'plane passing overhead and thinking, that's over, now what? Mike, left behind with me and no real home to give such a little fella, and no way, in the rather unsettled times of the approaching Mau Mau nastiness, of having him live with me in a (safari) tent, then his departure, (abroad), and finally, the long silence between us all."

cook and household staff, so we were set up and ready, hopefully, to start life anew.

"Christine began riding lessons on her new pony, 'Twilight', and we all enjoyed our dog 'Tosca' who unfortunately became a killer of goats, which cost us a fortune, but as the goats belonged to the cook, he was happy to be well paid for them. Christine was sent to a boarding school in the Nilgiri Hills. We felt the climate was too hot for her in Madras."

By March 1947 Charles was posted to Simla, a cool hill station where everyone longed to be. Wonderful views of the Himalayas, cool breezes and a good social life, Simla was the town where women and children and government officials were usually sent during India's monsoons, the very hot and steamy-wet times of the year. Servicemen during the war would hope to get away to Simla for well-earned leave. Mahatma Gandhi called it 'the unimaginable Simla Heights'.

"Previously, if you could get some leave from Burma in the hot weather, Simla was that piece of Heaven we all longed for. I was never that lucky then, as we were mostly on long range patrols chasing the Japanese, so it was with great pleasure I learned of my new posting," said Charles.

"Walking in Simla, just before dusk and into the Indian night, was a particularly beautiful time. The heady perfume of frangipani blossoms, flickering distant lights, the soft shuffle of sandaled feet as people enjoyed strolling in the cool evenings while punkas waved, fanning to cool the air further, and clouds of insects bumping endearingly into lamps, made the hours before dusk memorable.

"Scampering through the winding streets, at all times of the day, was a special breed of rusty-brown, Rhesus-type monkeys always chattering to each other as they sprang from tree-top to roof-top.

"Simla, a jigsaw puzzle of a town, seeming to tumble down mountains of pine and cedar trees was, for a century, transformed into one of the most important and powerful places on earth, for it was the summer capital of the British Raj, with a Tudor-styled stone town hall, a gazebo-like band-stand, the Victorian theatre; striking emblems of Britain.

"Viceregal Lodge, set on the peak of Observation Hill, was built almost like a castle with a large ballroom to hold hundreds.

"The whole township scene was magical, unlike my new archaic Indian State Forces headquarters manned by two full Generals, two full Colonels, a 2nd Lieutenant and me, a Major. It was a strange little unit, hardly to be found outside the MI5, but it was where the plotting of the break-up of India was taking place and a headquarters that was soon to write itself out of existence.

"Soon enough Josephine told me we were expecting our second child, due in November."

Charles, who enjoyed acting, (and, at times, an escape from his khaki uniform), began to take part in the plays which took place in the old and famous Gaiety Theatre, Simla's A.D.C. (Amateur Dramatic Club) which had always been an army officer's club that had kept its sun-never-sets outlook.

One piece in the Simla newspaper quoted, 'Charles Hayes, the lead in the play 'Quiet Weekend' was admirable and put across the male romantic character in a manner to overcome the hardiest feminine heart.'

In Noel Coward's 'Hay Fever,' (Josephine Hayes was wardrobe mistress), Charles took the part of 'Sandy Tyrel' who, it was reported in the newspapers, 'is ably played by Charles Hayes who succeeds by his set shoulders, and his movements generally, to convey that he is no mean amateur boxer.'[8]

---

[8] Charles seemed still to be following in Lord Baden Powell's footsteps (of Boy Scout fame), from the Gold Coast to Simla, India, (later changed to Shimla), where BP had taken part in acting at the Gaiety Theatre in 'The Geisha' in 1897.

Many famous people have appeared on Simla's Gaiety stage. Rudyard Kipling, during his years as a newspaper reporter/writer in Simla, 1883 to 1889, took part in a play 'Plot and Passion'. General Hunter-Weston, of World War 1, was in a play there in 1892.

A.D.C. records in Simla go back to 1887 when the Theatre was erected to commemorate Queen Victoria's Golden Jubilee, its auditorium a faithful scale version of the Royal Albert Hall in London, with only the acoustics being better in Simla.

Once the English had moved out of India, a Mr. Patel took over the old Gaiety Theatre insisting that the framed, original autographed sketches of famous actors who had taken part in plays, and which were hanging on the walls of the theatre, remained. In fact, before the theatre was handed over, the sketches were photographed and replaced, the originals being sent to London's Gaiety Theatre in The Strand where they may still be seen hanging on the walls there.

The reunited Hayes family move into their new house in Madras, India.

Charles and his daughter Christine with her dog 'Tosca', in their Madras garden.

Viceregal Lodge, Simla.

Charles takes a lead part in
a Noel Coward play at the
Gaiety Theatre, Simla

Charles and Jospephine Hayes (left) in Simla, dine in the Green Room after a Gaiety Theatre performance. At the table were the Mountbattens and author Compton Mackenzie.

SEVEN

I Was There

"Without knowing the force of words,
it is impossible to know men."
Confucius, c478-550

"THERE WAS A REMARKABLE SPECTACLE at our headquarters with all the toing-and-froing with Lord Louis Mountbatten, who lived a hundred yards away in the viceroy's palace," said Charles. "It was here, on June 6th,1947, that Mountbatten made the announcement to the world that his big decision to cut India into two parts by August 15th, 1947, was his only solution."

Said Mountbatten, "There cannot be just one India anymore. There seems to be no other way of keeping India together, so it has to be India and Pakistan. Muslims and Hindus simply cannot agree to live side by side." (Ghandi's thoughts, precisely).

Charles met with the newly-elected first Prime Minister of India, Jawaharial Nehru, who was head of the negotiating team, telling him of his concern about the Princeling States, which, he said, would be wiped out, and that the Maharajas would be no more; they would be abandoned. "All the treaties made with Queen Victoria would become null and void," Charles pointed out.

"For centuries the Indian Maharajas had controlled all the land and glory through a treaty with Queen Victoria, which had enabled them to get Arms. Suddenly, with the partitioning of Pakistan and India, their control would be taken over by the Indian Police Forces; the Maharajas being left with only their large estates.

"Britain did nothing to help, and I was very embarrassed," Charles admitted.

The morning after Mountbatten's announcement, (June 6th 1947), Maharajas, in all their splendour, with trimmed beards, turbans and rows of medals hanging on their military uniforms, arrived at Charles' desk to demand more Arms in order to fight India.

"It was an international incident," said Charles. "They were passed on to our General who said, quite calmly, to each Maharaja, 'Terribly sorry, old boy'."

The Maharajas, with millions of people kow-towing to them daily, stamped about on the office's wooden floor, saluting Charles and pleading over and over 'for Arms'. "They truly thought that Queen Victoria's treaty would enable them to get what they wanted. It was all very strange and, at the time, I didn't appreciate the seriousness of the situation. I knew so little of the Indian Army."

Charles was also somewhat embarrassed as he remembered how often the English-educated Maharajas, who played cricket and polo with the English officers, had invited him to partake of curry luncheons at their magnificent palaces. They had sat together on large, silk, embroidered floor cushions, each guest wrapped in a huge white towelling dressing gown, (to mop up the perspiration that flowed as they ate the hot, spicy food), where good friendly conversation and laughter between them came easily.

On August 14th, 1947,there was a special India Army Order sent out by His Excellency British Field Marshal Sir Claude John Eyre Auchinleck, G.C.B., G.C.I.E., C.S.I., D.S.O., O.B.E. Supreme Commander India and Pakistan, which read;

"With the transfer of power on the 15th August,1947, there will no longer be a Viceroy or Viceroy's House. All communications should be addressed to the Governor-General. The present Viceroy's House, New Delhi, and the Viceregal Lodge, Simla, will be re-designated

"Government House, New Delhi" and "Government-General's Lodge, Simla. This is the last India Army Order."

The stroke of midnight, that historical night, created a half-hour time difference between India and Pakistan, yet the Pakistan border was found to be only 250 kilometres away. (In the Urdu language, Pakistan means 'Land of the Pure'.)

It was then part of Charles' job to destroy the conglomerate mass of correspondence that had been sent between the Indian States Headquarters and all Indian Forces documentation, some from as far back as 1928, which he did, but Charles kept some of the signatures and ornate letterheads, many of which were inlaid with silver, gold, opal and mother-of-pearl.

"Nowhere else in the world would this type of luxury letterhead be printed except by Waterlow and Company Ltd., of London. The letterheads were far too beautiful to destroy."

In the six weeks between his first announcement that there would be a split up of India and the actual partition, Lord Louis Mountbatten, Governor General of India, chosen by the Labour Government of England, must have watched with great sadness as Simla, Britain's summer capital, became a killing area.

The great solution had gone so wrong. The utter joy of the pronouncement of Partition and Independence changed quickly to despair. Two countries were created out of old India (Pakistan) which meant that people had to choose between staying in the old India of Hindu religion, or moving to the new, Muslim, Pakistan (1/8th chopped off India); two opposing, horrifying upbringings which would make severe complications.

Charles, then, had to learn enough of the *Urdu* language to try to answer impossible questions and letters that, he said, 'went on and on.' Letters from the Maharajas contained such sentences as, 'Because of the lust of you Britons, I am what I have become. What is to become of us?' to 'we have no rations' and 'which way do we go?'

"Almost overnight, Simla streets became full of carnage. There was a total collapse of law and order during, and after, the partition. Communal violence resulted in a refugee population of 6,000,000 Muslims (in Pakistan) and 4,500,000 Sikhs and Hindus and, on the Indian side of the border, close to a million deaths.

"Walking to our offices with a fellow officer one morning, a Sikh, his kirpan, (a three-foot long sword), thrashing the air, rushed past us to chase a Muslim rickshaw boy. We took up the chase, but were too late to save the boy. We found the Sikh wiping the blood off his kirpan, the Muslim's head rolling on the street.

"We arrested the gleeful Sikh and took him to the police station. The following day, going back to give evidence, the new police officer, a Sikh, said to me, grinning, 'Sorry, Sahib, the prisoner he has escaped.'

"The first overcrowded train out of Simla, arranged by the Government of Britain to take Muslims to their new place to live, in Pakistan, was a disaster. A few miles down the track Sikhs had placed huge boulders across the line. When the train stopped, the Sikhs cut every passenger's throat. And so it went on."

On September 10th a dispatch from Simla to England was sent by Charles, which read:

"THE SHOCK of anything happening in Simla is too great for us to let the opportunity of broadcasting slip .The curfew of last night was continued throughout the day. European people don't mind so very much except those who have Muslim bearers for whom they now feel a moral responsibility.........Last night's episodes have become slightly clearer. It seems that the Muslim quarter of this small town was surrounded by Sikhs, who fired rifles indiscriminately into the wooden houses. This morning the Muslims retaliated by beating up a Hindu locality. At 3.p.m. this afternoon, a 'lifting of the curfew' took place. Five minutes later, all Muslim shops in the bazaar were looted and small boys were seen running about with brand new shoes and bales of cotton (cloth.). At 4p.m. the curfew was replaced. A man went along

Main Street shouting through a megaphone, and the locking of hefty wooden doors was soon the only sound to be heard...........I ducked when an armed policeman unslung his pistol and took a shot. I didn't see where it went. The officers of a company of paratroopers who have arrived here are billeted in Simla's Grand Hotel and are spreading the news, bravely, that they are just waiting to let fly at something, or someone. I'd like to be sure which way they are facing before I offer comment."

Four days later, on 14th September, 1947, another dispatch was sent by Charles, which read:

"YESTERDAY, I helped to organize the evacuation of starving, badly frightened people from the heart of the Muslim quarter; Simla families, the heads of which, only last week, were self-respecting clerks and Government servants. Since then they have lived in day and night fear of Sikh raids on their district and homes, of bombs thrown joyously, carelessly, by their Simla neighbours of many years. For days they dared not show themselves outside their houses – even for obtaining food for their families, knowing only too well that a murder in Simla is no longer unusual and that their Sikh brothers in Independence were hoping to arrange for more and more Muslims to die.........

Yesterday these people hurried, cowering, along the streets they knew so well, trusting only the British they knew but slightly and boarded a train to begin the long journey through the refugee camps to Pakistan. Simla has its killings, though numerous, but are on a small scale compared to the rest of Northern India. The news -- if it reports Simla at all -- says that the 'situation is under control' and with that obituary, the countless 'little men' die. The reason? The people say that these killings are only retaliations for the terror, which stalks in Pakistan. The Pakistani peoples kill, they say, for the same reason.

Today I have been detailed for night-guard duty at the Grand Hotel, which houses many British families. The object apparently is to repel an attack by a Simla Community because residents of the hotel have Muslim servants. This is not, on the face of it, a British quarrel, yet fundamentally the responsibility for this mass slaughter is ours. The world must come to regard the solution of the Indian problem, produced by Clement Atlee, (Deputy Prime Minister to Winston Churchill's War Cabinet), and his pack of backslappers, as wrong. Just as certainly, intervention of any sort by the British will be regarded as partisanship and will not be answerable not only individually, but in another outbreak of this not-yet discarded anti-British feeling." [9]

While on patrol Charles saw that Simla's railway station was piled high with rotting bodies. No one would bury them. Some of the people had died having been shot at by Sikhs from rooftops. Others had died of cholera, which was rife, as they waited hopefully for a train to take them to safety.

"Everyone thought, with the few Brits still around, there would be a 'cooling off'. But we were as nothing and Simla was suddenly a stupid place to be. We were told not to walk around in our uniforms. Britain had no authority to be there any more.

"I could see the solutions, and take notice of the huge event in history, but there was no impact that we could make.

"Sikhs were now wearing their kirpan swords openly, and cutting Muslims' throats daily. Mountbatten had left and so the 'ethnic cleansing' went on.

---

[9] Clement Atlee was the Dominion's secretary 1942/3. Between 1945/51 his government introduced the National Health Service in Britain and granted Independence to India, 1947 and Burma in 1948. In 1955 he accepted an Earldom, becoming Clement Richard Atlee, 1st Earl.

"With shots ringing out, and dying people -- some with cholera-- staggering along roadsides, our son, Michael Crawford Hayes, was born on November 2nd, 1947, in the Simla Hospital -- a hospital with a rusting, corrugated tin roof and armed guards standing at doorways."

Then a letter from the War office came for Charles releasing him from active military duty, commanded by the Army Council who expressed their thanks 'for the valuable service which he had rendered for his country at a time of grave national emergency.'

Two months later, after a horrendous Christmas season, all British Forces were informed that they could return with their families to England.

After Michael's Christening, in the Simla Cathedral, Charles wound up loose ends and looked round his office, a classic Edward Lutyens design, one of the architect's specials with the Georgian pillars outside, wondering if he would ever come back to India.[10]

Charles, glad to be on the move with his wife and two small children --Michael was barely three months old-- booked tickets for a ship that would take them to England. But first they had to return to Bombay, a long, tiresome journey he was dreading.

At Simla station, which clung to the side of a cliff at the bottom of town, a narrow train, renowned for taking at least seven hours to travel about 100 winding kilometres and through more than 100 tunnels from Simla to Kalka, at the base of the Himalayan foothills, awaited the Hayes family. But only Josephine took the train with little Michael while Charles went by road with Christine, driving with a friend from the London Zoo who's job it was to take a crated, small black bear back to England with him. It was believed, with the chaos in India, that indigenous animals might become endangered species. But the zoologist had not fixed the crate securely enough.

---

[10] When he arrived in Kenya, Charles found that Edward Lutyens, in 1929, had designed, as well as many other buildings, the Nairobi Law courts.

With a shout, the driver screeched to a halt and both Charles and the zoologist scrambled up the mountainside chasing the escaping young bear into a pine forest where they grabbed the animal by the back legs, securing it firmly back into the crate.

"The bear seemed to be laughing at us," said Charles who, with the zoologist, was exhausted. "Little Christine was wide-eyed and seriously interested in the whole procedure."

Meeting up with Josephine and baby Michael, the Hayes family began the next phase of their journey to Bombay.

"A small boy came to sell us food from a carved wooden tray containing a selection of samosas, small sweet cardamom cakes and toasted chickpeas, their flavour sharpened with fresh lime juice and marsala spices.

"I had no small change on me, only a 100 Rupee note," said Charles. "After buying a few small sweet cakes, the boy said, 'alright, Sahib, I will return with your change.' Of course he never did, so I hoped the 95 Rupees would keep his family in food for the next month."

And so it was with mixed feelings that Charles and Josephine gave their strange farewell to Simla, 'the summer capital of the British Raj'. For the Hayes family, it could be a new beginning; a hopeful reunion. But it was, they feared, near to closing time for them.

When Charles went to collect his belongings, stored since his move to Burma, in a warehouse at the Bombay docks, he found that a fire had broken out sometime before and the warehouse was no more.

"None of the Cameron Highlander's storage boxes, containing kilts, books and personal photographs, that had been stored ready for collection after the war, were left. I didn't bother to claim the insurance. The kilt didn't matter to me, as in all probability I would not be wearing it again and the pictures of my parents couldn't be replaced anyway."

On January 30th, 1948, the Hayes family boarded the SS Islanis to take them to now war-free England, but it was with a certain sadness that they heard the portside tanoy broadcasting the news that Mahatma

Gandhi, while walking to a prayer meeting, had been shot dead by a young Hindu fanatic, NathuRam Godse. (Three years later, the assassin was tried and convicted in Simla). Charles remembered how Ghandi had once said, "An eye for an eye is making the whole world blind."

One-month old Michael Crawford Hayes was christened at Simla Cathedral, December, 1947.

British Indian Passport photo, 1947

EIGHT

A New Beginning

*"Every man's work, whether it be literature, or music, or pictures,
or architecture, or anything else, is always a portrait of himself."*
Samuel Butler, 1835-1903

THE SHIP DOCKED in the port of Mombasa, Kenya, East Africa, where they learnt there was to be a delay for about four days.

The ship's captain suggested that Charles should take the family upcountry by train where they would be delighted, he said, with the wonderful country and the wild animals they would see on the way.

"Indeed it was a splendid sight to look at this beautiful Kenya and see how totally different it was to West Africa. Snow-topped Mount Kenya gleaming in the sunlight, plains game wandering in their thousands beneath flat-topped fever trees and the sight of waving, golden-red 'lion grass', coloured more vividly by an incredible sunset, made us wonder why on earth we were going to live in England.

"Realizing that we were utterly enchanted with East Africa, I went to the Army headquarters in Nairobi and asked if I may stay in Kenya. Permission was given and from there we were taken around the city and shown places of interest.

"There were no vacancies in the hotels, as it was Royal Agricultural Show week, so we travelled by train up to Nanyuki-- a town under Mount Kenya --where I had been offered a posting at the Infantry Training School in a small place named Burgeret. There we rented a house from June Hook. Her husband, the famous hunter Raymond Hook, lived two miles away with a Dutch woman known by everyone as

'Windmill'. A runner with a cleft stick kept communications open between husband and wife, which we thought amusing."

But Charles was not so amused when he saw how African staff members were treated. One day a huge handful of straw was pulled from the roof of a rondaval (round, African-style hut) belonging to one of the farm labourers, was thrown, heartlessly, in a heap outside his door 'to let him know that he is sacked', it was said. Charles did not approve of the way this was done.

"We rented our next house from another famous white hunter, Bunny Allen, known the world over by his natural charm, especially with women, and the single earring he wore, which was unusual in those days. But Bunny never left the house!"

Within a few months Charles Hayes resigned his commission in the army." The War Office, God bless it, accepted my resignation and I joined the administrative branch of the Colonial Service as a District Officer."

Charles was posted to the African district of Machakos, leaving his family, he said with a wry smile, "to the fate of Bunny Allen." And what a romantic fate for Josephine that turned out to be.

But Charles soon learnt that as far back as 1924, there had arrived in Kenya a couple who were to found a new kind of society, a reflection of Europe's latest haute monde.

There was a Scottish nobleman, Joss Hay, and his new wife Lady Idina, daughter of the 8th Earl de la Warr. Lady Idina's money had purchased for them a small farm and also a home, which became a port of call for a widening circle of friends who, once having made the long and arduous journey, stayed for days. In such welcoming circumstances, and amorous lifestyle, the area taken up by the new clique became known as 'Happy Valley'.

A river, tumbling from the Aberdare Mountains and running nearby the house, was said to 'flow with cocktails'.

Soon 'Happy Valley' achieved a reputation as a place where sex need not be limited by marriage and promiscuity was not only pleasurable but encouraged. For those who could keep up the pace, 'Happy Valley' was a different utopia and, as Kenya's popularity grew, more of Britain's post war elite joined them. Few though they were, the 'Happy Valley' crowd built around themselves a barrier of exclusivity. (Taken from the book *Oserian, a century of the Kenya story*, by Charles Hayes, 1997.)

It didn't take Charles and his wife long to realize that Kenya was well ahead of its time when they overheard someone ask, casually, "Are you married, or do you live in Kenya?"

In 1949, Bunny Allen's employer, Jack Soames, put Charles up for Muthaiga Country Club.

"I had just bought, from Clive Salter, a car which blew up on the red, very mucky wet murram (red soil) road as I was on the way to my interview at the club. Of course I arrived late, covered in oil and mud.

On meeting Salter I said, "You bastard, that second-hand Chevy panel van you insisted I had to have, has blown up!" Salter almost laughed himself off his seat. Nevertheless, I was invited to become a member of the prestigious Muthaiga Club."[11]

---

[11] White Hunter Bunny Allen died at his house in Lamu on January 2002. He was well over 90 years old.

Charles meets Bunny Allen in Lamu, Kenya Coast, in 1997.

Coastal fishermen with their early morning catch. (pic: CH)

The water catchment, Tsavo. (pic: CH)

Tsavo elephants on the move. (pic: CH)

NINE

Getting to Know the Country

"Time spent in reconnaissance is seldom wasted."
C.A.H.

INTERESTED IN THE HISTORY of his new country, Charles wanted to see for himself what it was like to walk oneself almost into a coma, in the heat and dryness of Tsavo, just as explorer Joseph Thomson had done in 1878.

Armed with Thomson's book, a map and a large bottle of water, he walked about 19 miles for most of the day. The book explained that Thomson and his group of 40 or so porters, (some of whom he found to be useless), climbed a hill looking for water in a deeply pitted rock. Thomson had found the natural rainwater catchment previously, while on his way from Tsavo to the Coast.

Charles recognised the rock, which was almost full of fresh rainwater.

"By the look of green grass around the place, I gathered there had been a rare storm, in this usually dry part of the country, just a short while before my getting there.

"Masses of game wandered, seemingly unconcerned, around me; Thomson's gazelles, (the explorer had named them), impala, zebra, giraffe, buck of all varieties and a herd or so of elephants minding their own business. I don't remember seeing any buffalo -- had there been I surely would not have forgotten, but I did see a lion lying sleepily on a hillock, taking no notice of me whatsoever. It was an interesting foot safari, which gave me a better insight into the work I was excited to start.

"A few weeks later there was a bit of a heart-stopping incident with lion in Longido, in Tanzania -- which eventually became a National Park.

"With two forestry officers, seated in an open Land Rover, we came across a pride of lion lying very near our vehicle track. When we started to move away slowly, one lioness began to follow, soon gaining on us. The land was full of bumps and warthog holes so we couldn't drive very quickly. At one moment the Landover stopped in its tracks, as did our hearts.

"We watched, transfixed, as the lioness crouched, ready to spring. The motor, thanks to our bright African driver, suddenly roared into action and the lioness, looking very cross indeed, slunk away into the long grass. The second officer said that he had been ready to throw himself out of the Landover, so that the three of us remaining could get away. We had no guns and we truly believed the pale-faced, shivering officer was not joking. I remember feeling not very much about the lion incident, believing, like the Maasai, that if you walk amongst wild animals without fear, they just carry on with their own lives. At least, I used to think so. 'Wild animals, especially lions, can smell fear,' so an old Maasai told me."

A film Company arrived in Kenya in the early fifties to make the film, 'King Solomon's Mines' from the famous book by Rider Haggard. Stewart Granger and Deborah Kerr were the main characters and while on a shoot at Machakos, the film company took over Charles' whitewashed government office.

About 50 Kenyans helped with the Metro-Goldwyn-Mayer production including Charles who was asked to go to and fro constantly to the little African post office to send, (and receive), telegrams from Granger to film actress Jean Simmons, with whom he was in love.

A grand charity ball, held when the film had finished, made money for a new Nairobi hospital.

As District Officer, Charles began to enjoy working in the small, dusty African town and its surrounds, about 65 kilometres northeast of Nairobi.

As soon as the film company had moved off to other East African locations, one of the first decisions he made was to get wells dug so that the poverty stricken Wakamba tribe, who were finding food and money scarce, could plant orange trees, beans, potatoes and maize, (corn), all of which would give them a nutritious diet. There had been a drought and older African men were losing interest in life, just sitting around chewing tobacco when they could get it. With the digging of new water wells, and seeds and trees to plant, life for the Wakamba began to take on a surge of hope. With crops and grass growing on land that had been almost bare, skinny cattle began to give milk again, so children gradually became healthier. Chickens were introduced and beehives were set up, offering a varied diet and a change from the goat meat the community had been surviving on.

A Doctor Igor Mann, who brought crates of chickens to sell to the 'Kamba' farmers, went into theatricals to push the idea of chicken-raising.

In his Polish accent he said, "Zee this bluddy njogoo, (cockerel)?" holding it upside down by its legs and wing-tips, African style, "it will make you pesa mingi (lots of money). Hey, wewe (you), hold this bluddy njogoo and see how lusty it is!" The farmers slapped their thighs and laughed and laughed and bought the 'bluddy' njogoo and the kukus, (female chickens). And they made money. Soon there were chickens running all over Machakos and eggs were plentiful.

"Then came the problem of what to interest the younger African boys." Charles went on, "with perfect timing, a letter arrived from Chief Scout, Brigadier-General Sir Godfrey D. Rhodes, who said that one of the urgencies in Kenya was to promote a stronger boy scout movement, suggesting I take over District Commissioner John Howard's interest in running a scout troop in Machakos, because John was leaving for a posting in Cambridge, England."

In a letter to Charles, John Howard said he thought that the scout idea was excellent and he hoped that the History of the Wakamba Charles was writing 'will come to fruition before long and please let me know of anything I can do to help it along', adding, 'I especially appreciate all your very hard work and the tactful manner in which you deal with the Wakamba.'

Sir Godfrey was general manager of the East African Railways and Harbours, but for much of his spare time, put thought and enjoyment into the scouting movement. His thinking was very much like Lord Baden Powell's.

"And so," said Charles, "that is how I became an Area Commissioner for Scouts in Machakos, probably a laughing stock by some of the hard-bitten settlers and D/O's, but for the young Africans, becoming a boy scout made a tremendous difference to their lives, and they needed a leader to show them the way.

"For these youngsters, who could rarely afford a complete scout uniform, they wore a 'kerchief' (necktie), a 'woggle' which they made for themselves out of hollowed-out bone and cut to one and a half inches deep, in order to keep their necktie in place, and a pair of khaki shorts, often old and ragged but scrubbed clean in the river. They were so proud of their uniforms and, because of them, became extremely disciplined, which impressed Lord Rowellan, Chief Scout of the World, when he visited us in Machakos from England.

"Accompanied by Sir Godfrey Rhodes, the two old 'Scouters' went to see Lord Baden Powell's grave set in a small cemetery near the Outspan Hotel, Nyeri, at the foot of the Aberdare mountain range. The grave stone has engraved on it a circle with a dot in its centre, meaning 'I have gone home', a sign that B.P. had invented for scouts, who were on a hiking or climbing expedition, to leave on the trail so that the rest of the troop would know where they had gone."

For a short time Charles was editor of a Scouts' newspaper, 'The Batian' -- the name given to Mount Kenya's highest peak.

"The newspaper was printed somewhere opposite the McMillan library in Nairobi," said Charles, "and I felt that if the scouting principles were accepted in Kenya, as they were for the rest of the world, then it would make a happy community."

The African Kamba community certainly seemed to be happier, but in Charles' personal life there was much stress and deep unhappiness.

His wife Josephine had run off to Geneva with a District Officer named Michael Hacking, (as Charles wrote to his mother, at that time, 'Josephine has scarpered, taking eight year-old Christine with her.')

Hearing through the 'bush telegraph' of his wife's planned departure, Charles 'kidnapped' young Michael and drove with him to his tented safari post where he stayed until Josephine had left the country.

Realising he couldn't keep his little four-year-old son indefinitely under canvas conditions, he returned to Machakos, making arrangements for Michael and his ayah, (nursemaid), to stay with friends who had a four-year-old daughter. This was a satisfactory arrangement while Charles was on safari.

In 1949, Charles' mother, Caroline Helena Hayes, who had been a widow since 1925, emigrated to Rhodesia, (today's Zimbabwe), the country about which her husband had spoken so fervently. Her younger son, Bill (Hayes), accompanied her, soon marrying a lady named Lois. Over the years they had four children, Gordon, Bryan, Lynne and another daughter who died of malaria when she was seven years old.

In 1951, rumours of a secret society, that spelt danger, were being circulated through the Kenya countryside.

The name of the society was Mau Mau.

Charles was glad to be offered a posting in the Department of Information in Nakuru, which was further up-country, nearer to the action he felt was bound to come.

Before returning his warrant as Area Commissioner for Scouts, Machakos area, Charles received, from the Boy Scouts Association, Kenya Branch, a letter from His Excellency, Lord Rowellan, after his visit. An extract went like this:

"A most encouraging rally and camp-fire. There was an excellent turnout with many of the young Africans coming over 100 miles. The Dance of Welcome and the display of crafts were excellent. I have seldom seen boys enjoy a campfire more. Hayes and Powell, the commissioners, allowed things to take their course yet never lost control of the situation. I wish one could see this loose but effective control more often exercised."

Before leaving for his new post in Nakuru, there were some strange goings-on in Machakos district, as reported in the small magazine, 'Kenya Today'.

"FIVE HUNDRED WITCHES attended a burning ceremony held recently in the Machakos district of 'Kamba country. But instead of the witches being burned, the flames consumed their paraphernalia including such magic charms as goat eyes, human fingernails, blood and soil. It was part of a district campaign to stamp out sorcery."

With the sneaky upsurge of Mau Mau (later known as the War of Liberation), and its dangers, it was with a certain amount of relief that Charles was asked by friends if they could take little Michael to England on the ship when they went on their three-month home-leave. Michael and their daughter of the same age would enjoy each other's company and make life easier for them all, it was agreed. So Mike went off to England with them.

"I missed the little fella very much," said Charles, "but knew that the times I'd be on safari, under canvas, would become more frequent, yet in the meantime it could give me breathing space in order to arrange a more secure household for us both by the time he returned.

"Another reason for letting him go to Britain was that a month or so earlier Michael had fallen onto a sharpened, wooden tomato stake in the garden, missing his eye by a fraction but leaving a scar which, I felt, should be looked at by an English doctor.

Michael would only be away for a short while, thought Charles.

But Michael was never returned to his father.

Three months later, excited at the thought of seeing his young son again, Charles went to meet the ship in Mombasa. But excitement soon changed to devastation when he found that his friends, while in England, had turned Michael over to his mother, Josephine, who held a Court Order for his return to her.

"On my way back to Nakuru, feeling utterly miserable and in shock, I thought out the whole scenario, coming to the conclusion, eventually, that children should rightfully be with their mother, especially if and when the mother married again, which would give the children another 'father'. It would only confuse the children, I thought unhappily, to call two men in their lives 'Dad'.

"With our divorce and Josephine's new marriage I bowed out, never again feeling at ease with my two children at being called, or even signing my name, 'Dad', until 14 years later when my third and last child, Caroline Rima, was born.

"It was an even sadder day, though, when I heard that my first children, Christine and Michael, had been given the new surname of 'Hacking', their step-father's name.

"I had neither been consulted nor had given permission for this change of name."

Charles, in later years, was very distressed to find that his first three grandchildren were also given the surname of 'Hacking'. "Their true name is Hayes," he said.

Three year-old Michael Hayes in Machakos, Kenya, 1950.

Young Michael enjoyed listening to *Munithyia wa Kyenza*, a Mkamba tribesman with his home-made musical instrument, the *mbembe*.

"I have gone home." Lord Baden Powell's grave in Nyeri, Kenya.
Below: Marker at Baden Powell's home in Nyeri. (pics: CH)

Charles' mother Caroline Helena Hayes, who lived in Zimbabwe, was, in 1978, aged 90.

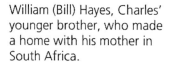

William (Bill) Hayes, Charles' younger brother, who made a home with his mother in South Africa.

A sleepy Kenyan cheetah. (pic: *Africana Magazine*)

Rhinos, although dangerous, have poor eyesight, so keep the wind blowing in the opposite direction when you see them!
Zebra amongst whistling thorn trees on the Kenya plains. (pics: CH)

Cheetah on the alert. (Pic: R. Bjorndala for *Africana Magazine*).

Leopard in a 'sausage' tree. (pic: *Africana Magazine*)

TEN

Phase Two

"Life is far too important a thing ever to talk seriously about."
Oscar Wilde

ENTERING A NEW PHASE, Charles began to make arrangements for starting his new assignment as Provincial Information Officer, Rift Valley, in the up-country town of Nakuru.

He had already taken shares in EAPEX (East African Photographic Exchange), which later became the EA Press Exchange (and later still, The Charles Hayes Company Ltd.).

Charles had bought his shares from Freda Yowell, widow of Freddie Yowell, who had lost his life while photographing crocodiles. His boat had overturned, losing all photographic equipment. Freddie, while trying to swim to a riverbank, (somewhere in East Africa), was eaten by one of the huge, sharp-toothed reptiles he had hoped to capture on film.

Returning to Machakos for a few days, in order to sort out some business accounts, Charles was walking through the bush on his way to Athi River, where he was to meet a group of Africans. Rounding a clump of thick scrub he saw, suddenly, a blonde-haired, bare-breasted woman sitting on the rough earth of an African path. She was painting a portrait of a young, also bare-breasted, African woman of the Kamba tribe.

"The artist seemed not in the slightest embarrassed as I approached her, but in deference to me, I think, she very casually put on a sun-faded sleeveless shirt that had been lying on her lap. I didn't know who she was and we didn't stop to introduce ourselves fully, but I found later that she was Joy Adamson who had married George Adamson in 1944: her third husband. They lived near Isiolo, in the NFD (Kenya's Northern Frontier District), for much of their time, where they cared for the wild lions they had befriended."

By the early 60's, by which time Charles was editor of '*Africana*,' a glossy, wildlife conservation magazine, (an off-shoot of the *Nation Group* of newspapers), he knew the Adamsons well. They were then becoming famous with their books, '*Born Free*' and '*Living Free*.' Many of Joy's portraits of Africans, and her beautiful paintings of African wild flowers, hang today in Nairobi's Museum. Money from the sale of any of her paintings went towards Kenya's Wild Life Fund and later, 'The Elsa (lion) Fund'.

After a meeting with Kenya farmer and politician, Sir Michael Blundell, Charles joined the Rift Valley Club in Nakuru. Sir Michael wanted Charles to re-join the government as a D.O. again but Charles declined graciously as he was already enjoying his new position as Provincial Information Officer.   He had also been appointed assistant editor to the East African Literature Bureau, a company that was just beginning to publish in the Kiswahili language.

"No other publisher was doing this then, so it interested me very much. Writer Elspeth Huxley was on the board of the East African Literature Bureau, which financed the Swahili magazine *Tazama*, meaning 'Look', first published in 1952."[12]

In February 1952, Charles, then editor of *Tazama*, was following the story of Princess Elizabeth who, with her husband Prince Phillip, had

---

[12]   Sir Michael Blundell, born in London, emigrated to Kenya in 1925,involving himself in settler politics. He was a member of Legco (Legislative Council) 1948-63, and leader of Europeans 1954. He became Kenya's Minister of Agriculture 1955-9 and again 1961-3. He broke with the white group to support political change involving black Kenyans and was much vilified for this. However, he was an essential bridge between the white dominated colonial years and the black majority rule of independent Kenya (1964).

Author Joy Adamson of "Elsa the Lion' fame. (pic: M.B. Ltd.)

arrived on a five-day safari to Kenya. After a non-stop schedule, their final two days were to be spent at 'Treetops', a beautiful lodge built in a large fig tree that grew deep within the cool, Aberdare forest.

Baboons arrived at the Lodge every day at teatime, jumping about on the uppermost tree branches and leaping onto the shaded verandah where visitors fed them left-over biscuits and honey-topped slices of toast.

Although a state of emergency was not actually declared until the following August, there was a question of utmost security as the African Mau Mau movement was just starting and there was a problem with the Press, who had been told that no photographs were to be taken of the Royals' private visit.

Nevertheless, by early February, about 20 photographers and journalists, including Charles Hayes, had already booked into the nearest hotel - The Outspan, in Nyeri township.

On February 5th, 1952, there was a certain amount of stress while staff at Treetops awaited the arrival of the Royal couple, who had been staying at Sagana, Kenya's nearby Royal Lodge.

At 1:30p.m., discordant trumpeting sounds echoed loudly through the forest so that everyone wondered who would arrive at 'Treetops' first. But they all arrived together -- 50 elephants and the Royal couple. The princess had never seen an elephant in the wild, and there were some anxious moments until Her Highness had been safely escorted up the ladder and seated comfortably on the verandah at the top-of-the–Tree.

After dinner that evening, with a false moon beaming down on the salt lick, the royal party watched rhino, buffalo and various antelope wandering below them and listened, enthralled, to the high-pitched screams of tree hyrax and the eerie chuckle of hungry hyenas. Elephants roamed beneath the tree for much of the night, giving the royal visitors, wrapped in blankets with, maybe, a glass of warm brandy in their hands

--the high altitude makes air there very cold at night-- a perfect view of the enormous creatures.

Leopard, and other forest animals, also came to visit the salt lick and drink at the pool between the hours of dusk and early dawn, thrilling the sleepless onlookers.

But the night of the royal couple's arrival also brought very sad news. The Princess was informed, early next morning, that during the night her father, King George 6th, had died peacefully in his sleep.

At that moment Her Highness, Princess Elizabeth, had become Her Majesty, the Queen of England.

An early morning plane flew the royal couple over the Kenya border to Kampala, in Uganda, where they immediately boarded a plane to London.

"As soon as the news broke," remembered Charles, "I rushed down to the *Tazama* office, within the *East African Standard* newspaper office in Nairobi, and saw editor David McDowell-Wilson. The *Reuter* news announcement that the King had died came through the 'ticker-tape', half-inch wide paper strips that contained world news that most days ticked away, landing in rolled heaps on the floor.

"This news was red hot. With the *Tazama* and *Standard Newspaper* staff we threw out the *Standard* front page for that day, replacing it at once with the large headline, "The King is Dead. Long Live the Queen", followed by the story of her few hours safari in Kenya's Aberdare forest, with other headlines such as; "She went up (to 'Treetops') a Princess and came down a Queen". The newspaper hit the streets by midday."

The 16-page *Tazama* magazine quickly became of great interest to Africans. Weekly articles included a 'Love' serial, written by Charles and translated into Kiswahili by an African journalist. There was a full page on sewing and crafts, a half-page on Kenya history. English 'lessons' were very popular as was a column of 'jokes' in each language.

"Advertising began to pick up under the supervision of (Mrs.) Althea Tebutt," said Charles, "and we were all delighted when Phillips Bicycles, Boot's Chemists and Brylcream, (for the hair), began advertising regularly. Many African youths liked Brylcream so much, (the sweet smell and the creamy texture), that they admitted to spreading it onto slices of bread for a midday snack!"

From Andrew's Liver Salts to Honeydew cigarettes --with a picture of an elephant on the packet --advertising began putting the newspaper in funds.

"But there was a time when Mrs. Tebutt and myself had to take turns in tossing up a coin to see which one of us would get a salary for that month."

In one issue Charles wrote the story 'Kenya's Country of the Blind', accompanied by several photographs, which caught the attention of many Kenya readers. A shortened version went like this....

"IF YOU GO amongst the Suk people of northwest Kenya, your heart drops. Hundreds of them are blind.

Across the hot sands of the area, in the hill forests and small settlements of this nomadic, cattle-loving tribe, the older people stretch out their walking sticks, feeling the way they used to see.

Doctor Robert Alexander McKelvie, a Scots-born, Kenya Medical Department eye specialist, went to Suk country to examine the situation. The Suk people were suspicious of services supplied by Government, preferring their own primitive cures, which, more often than not, did not work. Yet Dr. McKelvie reckoned that he could cure a great deal of blindness, not in the expensive surgeries of the Colony's main towns, but by working in the primitive conditions of the East Suk District.

At first the Suk people were unwilling to submit themselves to the 'white man's magic', but when the bandages were taken off the eyes of the first trusting patients, whoops of joy came from the old people known to have been blind for years, then much of the cautiousness disappeared.

On one of his long journeys McKelvie found people waiting for him at the side of a track. They were blind and had been on their way to his encampment. He examined them, operating on the spot using, as a surgical table, two planks of wood set between the bodies of trucks in his convoy, and a large cotton sheet spread over the top for protection from the fierce sun.

The 'restorer of sight' then went on to look at Samburu country where, in the hot, dry conditions there was a tradition of smearing cattle grease and rancid butter on bodies, which, of course, attracted flies and therefore blindness.

In three weeks he had examined 896 blind Samburu, working from 7.a.m. until darkness fell. In the next village he operated on 278 people in the 32 days he was able to stay there. All of them can see today. I talked to some of the Africans sitting outside Dr. McKelvie's tiny hospital in a small administrative centre. They were not frightened of the ordeal which was to come, and all now felt quite safe in the quiet, white man's hands. To him, a diseased eye, even if it belongs to a criminal--or a duped Kikuyu who has sworn to kill others--is something that he must do his best to cure. And many Africans in Kenya testify to the fact that his best is a miracle."

Charles, in his spare time, was connected to a local professional theatre, the 'Donovan Maule Studio Theatre' in Nairobi, and enjoyed acting in several productions.

"I had promised to take part in the play "Blythe Spirit" after my return from visiting Bulawayo, South Africa, where my brother Bill and my mother lived.

"A month or so before, I had bought a 64-acre lot in Timau, Kenya, at an altitude of about 10,000 feet on the slopes of Mount

Kenya, that I wanted my mother and brother to have. I hoped they would come to Kenya to live, so went to talk it over with them."

During his time in South Africa, Charles, always interested in politics, (especially what was happening or about to happen in South Africa), met with Joshua Mqubuko Nyongolo Nkomo who had been elected Chairman of the Southern Rhodesian A.N.C. (African National Congress) in 1951. Nkomo had been educated at Fort Hare College in Natal where he had first become interested in the ANC.

Charles also met up with Harry Mwaanga Nkumula, elected President of N.R.A.N.C. (Northern Rhodesia African National Congress). From these two men, and many other Africans, Charles obtained ideas that would make news in East Africa.

"Mau Mau, known by Kenyan Africans as the 'War of Liberation,' had well and truly started. We could all see it boiling up. It was a political problem. My brother, having lived in South Africa for some time, could only see it as a shooting war. I couldn't get along with Bill at that time, so I punted around a lot talking to Africans, realizing that Joshua Nkomo and his friends, the tops of the African political world, were with me, telling me the future plan of Africa. I met all the leaders who pointed me towards recognising a messenger system that was travelling down through the spine of Africa."

ELEVEN

A Force to be Reckoned With

"It is not a writer's business to hold opinions."
W.B Yeats

BY THE TIME Charles had left South Africa to arrive back in Nairobi, a terrible news story was headlining local newspapers.

Early one morning there was the horrific Mau Mau murder of Doctor Esme Ruck, her husband and their little son in their up-country house in the Kinangop.

Immediately Charles was in his car, which awaited him at the airport, driving to the murder scene, two hours away.

"It was absolutely dreadful," said Charles. "Dr. Ruck was still lying on the garden path. Her husband was stretched out with a sheet over his head in the doorway of the house. Upstairs was another terrible scene. The young Ruck son had been murdered in his bed. The whole family had been chopped up by two-edged simis or pangas (large knives), the type every African owns.

"It was believed that the Ruck family was loved by their African staff. Dr. Ruck administered to any African who needed medical treatment, nursing women though illnesses and childbirth, and African staff were known to have loved the little son. Yet the whole Ruck family was killed and it had happened because of Mau Mau oathings during Kenya's 'Emergency'.

"It is harder to kill the thing you love than the thing you hate, went the Mau Mau brainwashing, so when an oathed Mau Mau member was told to kill, he had to prove that he had the courage to do it, whoever it might be. If instructions were not carried out, he felt the

93

potent oath he had taken would be powerful enough to cause him to die himself."

A confidential report on Mau Mau oathing ceremonies and activities was sent to European government department heads to help explain how members of Mau Mau operated. Here is a much-shortened version:

"IN VIEW of the recent launching by Mau Mau of a campaign to re-oath its adherents, and to enclose in its net an ever-greater number of African followers, not only of the Kikuyu community and of the increasing bestiality of the oath ritual, it is timely and necessary to appreciate anew the significance of Mau Mau ceremonial practices and to review the extent and type of atrocities perpetrated by members of this movement.

From time to time, much has been written about the significance of tribal oaths, some 70 in number, in the life of the WaKikuyu still held as he is in the grip of pagan superstitions and ideologies.

The originators of the Mau Mau War of Liberation chose the more powerful features of these many oaths to ensure that the Mau Mau version was supremely powerful -- as it has since proved to be, despite the fact that in three ways it transgresses Kikuyu custom, which prohibits the administration of oaths by night, by force and to women. The original aim of Mau Mau, as expressed in the words of the oath, was secretly to unite, discipline and foster political consciousness amongst the Kikuyu, with the ultimate objective of satisfying the political aspirations of its leaders, by force if necessary. The terms of the oaths were as follows:

(a) If I ever reveal the secrets of this organization, may this oath kill me.

(b) If I ever sell or dispose of any Kikuyu land to a foreigner, may this oath kill me.

(c) If I ever fail to follow our great leader, Kenyatta, may this oath kill me.

(d) If I ever inform against any member of this organization, or against any member who steals from the European, may this oath kill me.

As the Mau Mau campaign gained strength, and the advocates of violence came to the fore, the terms of the original oaths were amended to include the following new clauses, inter alia:

(e) If I am sent to bring in the head of any enemy and I fail to do so, may this oath kill me.

(f) If I fail to steal anything I can from a European, may this oath kill me.

(g) If I ever receive any money from a European as a bribe for information, may this oath kill me.

(h) If I refuse to help in driving the Europeans from this country, may this oath kill me.

With the advent of these new terms there came an increase in acts of violence by Mau Mau.

The oaths, so far described, are the general or third grade oaths from which no Kikuyu man, woman or young person is exempt. Its effect has been to create a mass of violent-minded, often bewildered people, chained by superstition and fear to the commands of their unscrupulous leaders. In the early days the ritual was primitive but not bestial, its symbolism alone being sufficiently powerful to bind initiates to the terms of the ghastly oath. In more recent times bestial practices have embellished the ritual in certain areas, particularly in Meru, Mount Kenya area.

With the launching of the violent campaign a stronger, or second grade, oath was administered.

Only leading political agitators take a second-grade oath, but two new versions have been devised for terrorists. The first called for the 'sacrifice of blood and the blood of Kikuyu for freedom'.

The second, the 'gathaka' or 'forest oath', was administered by forest leaders to their followers, and a third, was the 'Batuni', a battalion, or platoon oath. By taking the Batuni, a soldier recruit becomes a full-blooded terrorist. Batuni oaths are:

(a) To burn European crops and European-owned cattle. If ordered to kill, to kill no matter who is to be the victim, even one's father or brother.

(b) When killing, to cut off heads, extract eyeballs and drink the liquid from them.

(c) Particularly to kill Europeans.

It must be seen that the terms of the Mau Mau have become increasingly more violent and blood thirsty, envisaging even the killing of father by son and brother by brother. The only possible deduction to be drawn from the details of the bestiality and perversion connected with the ceremonies is the horrible one that we are now faced in Kenya with a terrorist organization composed of those who have forsaken all moral codes in order to achieve the subjugation of the Kikuyu tribe and the ultimate massacre of the European population of the Colony.

That these terrible rituals and oaths drive the participants to honour their vows is only too apparent from the lurid list of atrocities committed to Mau Mau.

- Exhumation of bodies and eating the putrefying flesh; - Drinking human blood; - Victims held down while their heads are sawn off slowly with pangas; - Maiming of cattle by hamstringing; - Cutting off ears of persons who have not taken the oath, so as to identify them in the future as (British) Government loyalists.

Growing up side-by-side with and immersed in these horrors is the new generation of Kikuyu youth, which ever since reaching the age of reason has been indoctrinated with a hatred of the European, a fanatical admiration for Kenyatta, and a disregard for parental and tribal authority. These young men are the backbone of the 'War of Liberation' and they owe no allegiance to the ordinary dictates of either Christian or pagan ethics. Such then is the problem of Mau Mau.

The gradual extermination of terrorists will, in the end, undoubtedly sway the majority of the WaKikuyu against terrorism as a means of achieving an end. There will remain, however, the need to lead the debased and unruly youth of the community to a better way of life. Normal means of rehabilitation are unlikely to succeed until the common law of discipline had been instilled and is obeyed."

"There were more terrible, degrading oaths and detailed confessions, enough to make a person sick with horror," said Charles, "so the Europeans, whatever their job in Kenya, from farmers to Government employees, set to work in trying to rid the country of Mau Mau.

"British planes came in to try to flush out terrorists by dropping bombs into thick forest areas where Mau Mau gangs lived and British troops arrived to help. Even Ugandan soldier, Idi (Dada) Amin, who had joined the Kings African Rifles in 1946 and had attended O.C.T.U,

(Officer Cadet Training Unit) at England's Sandhurst Military Academy, fought with the British army during Kenya's Mau Mau uprising. It was a very strange and stressful time for Kenya."

It was at that time Charles handed in his Italian-made handgun for safe keeping under Police Amnesty Kenya. The gun had been given to Charles by a General in the Indian State Forces at the end of the war. "It was the last firearm I owned."

Newspaper editors from many countries started to bombard Kenya writers for updated, intimate stories about Mau Mau. Charles wrote a piece for the *Bulawayo Chronicle*, (then Rhodesia), in December 1953, headlined;

'Some Rites of Mau Mau Officers. Promotion Depends on Perversion', which went like this:

"IN THE BACKGROUND among the Kikuyu, power politics reign supreme in the new excesses to which Mau Mau oath-takers are expected to subscribe.

There is no newspaper in the world that would publish the full list of the oath forms and all that civilized man can do is to forget the memory of them. Yet it is against this backdrop that (our) screening teams are working and security forces fight.

There are probably few people in the world who remain unaware that membership of the Mau Mau organization is attained by swearing an oath in a form somewhat resembling Kikuyu customs.

In the eyes of most people the oath is designed to ensure allegiance to a cause; yet it is becoming increasingly clear that the oaths are not merely the mumbo jumbo of a secret society, but are part of a deliberate attempt to bring the Kikuyu to its knees.

The playwrights and producers of the oathing ceremonies appear to have given free rein to their pornographic imaginations; the higher-grade oaths no longer bear any resemblance to tribal custom. What is left is a group of Calibans; a mass of honourless thugs.

The world may care to remember that women have been lashed to trees, raped and ravaged at times when ancient tradition decreed that no man should have contact. They, too, have been part of the stage-production of the play, which turns men into inhuman automatons.

You may become a Major -- or the treasurer who takes a cut on Mau Mau collections -- if you will eat the brain of a dead man. In a recent Supreme Court case, witnesses told how men were ordered to exhume a body, dead for 14 days, and eat the stinking flesh. Women, like their men folk, are the pawns in the game of producing a race to which no crime, no indecency, is any longer offensive.

Charles summed up his article, of which only part is printed here:

CAN MEN SURVIVE the onslaughts of their moral fibre; can the garbage of the ceremonies leave no deeper mark than that of loyalty to the killer movement?

Certainly it is no wonder that men who have been rescued by our screening teams from this morass -- men who have been allowed to get on their feet again on firm and decent soil -- begin to fight back against the men who have bid for power at any cost."

In the same newspaper the editor headed a column; 'Power Politics: Test of Strength', adding;

"Charles Hayes, in his authoritative article on Mau Mau, the War of Liberation, recalls that the middle months of 1952 saw the growth in Kenya of political thuggery when, in the Nairobi African areas, muscle-men and gang-bosses began their campaign against anything European in origin. One of the first points of attack was against the wearing of European-type clothes; the orders were that hats would no longer be worn and mobs waited at vantage points to snatch and burn a 'trilby' hat from the head of African passers-by. Women were ordered to return to wearing the yellow and blue old-time shuka cloth and there was a list of 35 British-owned Nairobi firms, which were the targets in plans to break the Colony's economy. Men of other tribes succumbed to the power politics of the Kikuyu; fear of savage reprisals seized the imagination of Nairobi dwellers, not that a man cared so much for his own, but the threats included attacks upon his family who were often defenseless against the swift killing by armed men to whom conscience is just a word in the English language."

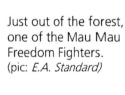

Just out of the forest, one of the Mau Mau Freedom Fighters.
(pic: *E.A. Standard)*

TWELVE

Discussion versus Violence

"Where is the wisdom we have lost in knowledge?
Where is the knowledge we have lost in information?"
T.S. Eliot

CHARLES TOOK TO THE ROAD with those of his African staff who could speak the Kikuyu, Kiswahili and English languages, setting up mobile cinemas to attract African crowds.

Through loudspeakers, fixed up by Jeff Baker of Baker Radios in Nakuru, Charles and his staff gave out information about Mau Mau, reporting news of what was happening within the hour. They even talked about help for new farming methods once Mau Mau members had given themselves up, and often used theatrical effects to get important points across.

"Jeff had just put in a speaker system for Lord Egerton at his baronial hall in nearby Njoro. It was the very first 'all round' sound in Kenya. Lord Egerton and the Honourable Nellie Grant, (writer Elspeth Huxley's mother), had made it possible for Africans to become students at the Edgerton Agricultural College, in the Rift Valley.

"With Jeff's expertise, our set of mobile cinemas travelled through the Mau Mau hot-spot areas of Kenya. A sound system bellowed forth our anti-Mau Mau messages from a little wooden office in Nakuru's main street, making the whole set-up a tremendous attraction for Africans who were eager to listen, to learn and to send messages back to Mau Mau members to 'come out of the forests'."

In a letter to his mother, Charles wrote:

"A PART OF THIS Information Department is to try to 'sell' the Europeans (the whites), in the settled areas of the White Highlands, as they are called, the idea that you cannot forever rule Africa with guns.

The country here is in a bit of a muddle, one way and another, and it is only now that the 'Europes' are realizing just the mental hold which Mau Mau has obtained. I told your Bulawayo Rotary Club, or was it the Twenty-One Club, the very same thing when I visited you last, when no one here in Kenya believed that a few Africans could give the run-around to British troops for more than a minute or two.

Then, on March 26th, 1953, the Lari Massacre happened; a night when African Mau Mau members attacked, killed and maimed Christian-thinking Kikuyu villagers who were not interested in taking oaths. Over 100 WaKikuyu, of the loyal Chief Luka, were butchered by insurgents of the Mau Mau secret society.

Men, women and children of their own tribe were decapitated, disembowelled and mutilated. Pregnant women's stomachs were cut open and the unborn fetus' flung into their faces. Domestic animals were either ham-strung, or their back legs chopped off, leaving the animals to bleed to death."

On the same night, a few miles away, Naivasha's police station in the Rift Valley was attacked, Africans killing Africans. Prisoners were set free, 47 weapons and approximately 4,000 rounds of ammunition were stolen and three African policemen were killed. Charles recalled, "there was a horror story to be found in the newspapers every day."

THIRTEEN

Looking Back. Moving Forward

"Minds are like parachutes –
they only function when they are open."
Sir James Dewar, 1842-1932

BACK IN THE EARLY DAYS of 1950, Charles had met an African
of the Kikuyu tribe who had been educated by Scottish missionaries and
was editor of the Kikuyu Central Association's newssheet
'*Mwigwithania.*' This African had been living in England to attend the
London School of Economics, (all the while writing his book, *Facing
Mount Kenya*), and, as president of the anti-colonial movement, had
begun to make his mark as a major spokesman.

Kamau Ngengi Jomo Kenyatta had worked in England at various
jobs during World War II and had married an English woman who gave
birth to their son, Peter. For Charles, Kenyatta was a man of
extraordinary interest and intellect for on Kenyatta's return to Kenya
from England in 1946, he had been elected President of the K.A.U.
(Kenya African Union).

Four years later, in early 1950, Charles made an appointment to
talk to him.

"As there was tension building up in Kenya, with the talk of a
secret society rumoured to be led by an African, Jomo Kenyatta and I
agreed to meet after dark in an Asian duka, (small shop), in River Road,
Nairobi, to talk things over in confidence.

"By the light of an oil lamp -- there was no electricity in that area
–and only a conglomeration of cats as our audience, we sat on rice-
sacks talking and passing a bottle of cheap 'Beehive' brandy between

us. We talked all night and by the time the sun promised to rise, Kenyatta got up from his seat on the rice sack and, staggering only slightly towards the old wooden shuttered door, made his farewells with a wide smile. We had made friends and he had given me a story.

"As for me, I couldn't get up. He was a better drinker than I."

Towards the crescendo of Mau Mau, when an Emergency was declared in Kenya, Kenyatta was tried and, some believed, found guilty of what was later proved to be perjured evidence. He was sentenced for 7 years and jailed at Lokitaung, in a remote corner of Kenya's northwest, near the junction of Ethiopia and Sudan, after which he was detained for a 2-year period at hot and dusty Lodwar.

Charles remembered the evening before Kenyatta was arrested, when they had sat together on a rock within wading distance in the river at Thika, some miles outside Nairobi, where they had talked until dusk, Kenyatta thinking out loud about a future Kenya.

In 1954, one year after the Lari Massacre, Charles went to talk to the villagers there. A young African girl, with only one arm, sat looking out into the distance as Charles talked to her.

"What do you remember about the night of the massacre?" he asked gently.

Shyly, the girl who had been responding went quiet when an older African walked by.

"You see that man," she whispered, "He is the Kikuyu who chopped off my right arm the night Mau Mau attacked our village."

Charles realized there was no hatred coming from this girl-child, just deep sadness and a lack-lustre in her young eyes.

It seemed that victims and attackers had begun to live side-by-side as if little had happened to make it otherwise.

Although people in Kenya were uneasy, Nairobi nightclubs were open, and dance bands sounded loud and clear throughout the city, sending depression fleeing for at least a short time.

Jomo Kenyatta, 1952
(Pic: *Tazama* Magazine)

Many white Kenyans wore a gun slung round their waists. One night, when an African band was making life in the city a happier place by throbbing out its irresistible beat, Charles went to Nairobi's 'Travellers Club' for a drink with some of his friends. One of Charles' magazine journalists was playing the drums. Tom was a Coastal African, a newspaper writer/ translator who put the cliffhanger love stories Charles wrote and serialised for *Tazama* magazine into the Kiswahili language.

"In the club that night," Charles remembered, "was Jane Wyneaton, wife of the D.C. (District Commissioner) Naivasha. Well into her cups, she demanded that Tom play the drums faster.

"Becoming increasingly frustrated at the slow pace, she pulled out her .38 and shot straight through the drum. Unfortunately the bullet also went through Tom's leg. She looked at Tom, saw that he wasn't dead and said imperiously, "you're all right NOW, aren't you?"

Charges were never laid. She was a white woman, a D.C.'s wife and anyway, she said, she didn't mean to shoot at his leg.

"A few weeks later I received a post card from Tom who had flown off to Edinburgh, Scotland to recuperate, saying, 'This place isn't so different from Nairobi except there are not so many white people here!'"

As a bachelor Charles dated many women friends during his time in Nairobi and Nakuru. While he was sharing a house with a District Officer, he invited one of his female friends for dinner, warning her that the man who shared his house made appalling slurping sounds when eating soup.

"She looked suitably understanding," said Charles.

"Nevertheless, when dinner was served I tensed myself for the inevitable soup-slurping. Indeed it came with a noisier slurp than usual. I looked at the girl, hoping she was not too disgusted, but found to my horror that it was she who was making this unholy noise.

"That was the end of what might have become a budding relationship."

FOURTEEN

A New Romance

'Life is short; opportunity fleeting; experience
treacherous; judgement difficult.'
Hippocrates

BY mid-1952, Kenya's V.O.K. (Voice Of Kenya) radio was little more than a 'whimper in the wilderness' laced with propaganda through the historic, stormy days marking the Mau Mau Emergency. But the message the Information Department managed to broadcast was confined to a limited and privileged few – those who could afford to own a radio receiver.

Language, in a land of many tribal dialects, was only one of the obstacles in sending radio messages throughout Kenya.

Charles had still, at times, been taking part in Donavan Maule Studio Theatre plays, but decided that he was too tired to rush up and down the 90 or so miles from Nakuru to Nairobi for rehearsals. He kept his promise to help out in just one more play.

The leading lady, with whom he had to learn his words, was Jean Parnell, a professional actress who had arrived from London to Kenya, with actor friend Basil Hurle-Hobbs, to join the Donovan Maule Studio Theatre.

Basil, who had been a Fleet Air Arm pilot during the war, and Jean bought an old R.A.F. wood and fibre 'spotter' plane they named 'The Gypsy Queen', in which, it was planned, Basil would pilot them to Kenya within a scheduled 10 days.

En route to East Africa, and after many serious problems, the plane burned up after landing in the desert sands of Wadi Halfa, (later to be consumed by the waters of the new Aswan Dam). It had taken the couple five and a half months to get that far.

Jean and Basil had air tickets sent out from England enabling them to board a B.O.A.C. (British Overseas Airways Corporation) Solent flying boat which took them to Kenya, coming in to land at a wooden jetty near Crescent Island on Lake Naivasha, the largest of a string of lakes in the Great Rift Valley. They were taken then by motor launch to the beautiful 600 acre, volcano-rimmed Island where reception huts were located, then driven to Nairobi.

The B.O.A.C. operation had taken over from the Imperial Airways Sunderland Flying Boat service, which used to fly local Kenyan passengers and settler children, to and from their vacations and English and South African schools.

It was during the Donovan Theatre rehearsals that Charles and Jean decided, after the romantic play had ended, they would get married, which they did in March, 1953.

Charles marries actress Jean Parnell in Nairobi. March 1953.

Returning to Nakuru, Charles continued with his work as Provincial Information Officer and editor of the Swahili magazine *Tazama*, (*Look*), published by the East African Literature Bureau, while Jean, who after marrying Charles had given up her acting career, was offered a position as Program Producer in the African Broadcasting Club (A.B.C.).

Her Kiswahili was at that time, she admitted, 'painfully limited', but when on her first day she was told, casually, to produce and present an ABC program for African women for that afternoon, she accepted the challenge, preparing a script in record time.

The English actress was 'reduced to hysteria' before the day was through, but women listeners enjoyed her program.

Radio was one of the few weapons used in order to fight Mau Mau. Often travelling throughout the country, Jean gave away what were called 'saucepan' radios, which were round, cheaply made in aluminium, and more importantly, were highly effective.

Tazama picture features the saucepan radio.

Jean stayed as Program Organiser until 1957 when she and Charles launched *Andrew Crawford Productions Ltd.*, in Jeevanjee Street, Nairobi, a recording company specializing in radio and television commercial productions for East Africa and the offshore Islands. Charles named the company after his own middle name, (Andrew), and his Grandmother's maiden name, (Crawford), which was also the middle name of Charles' son Michael.

Jean was undoubtedly one of the pioneers of Kenya radio.

Between broadcasting 30-second news spots for BBC's '*The World Today*' and reporting on the Mau Mau activities which had most of East Africa, (Kenya, Uganda and Tanzania), listening, Charles was enjoying his new promotion as The Head Of The African Services, (THOTAS), Department of Information, Nairobi.

As an outstanding personality in the media and literary scene, and with a 'golden voice', Charles was frequently 'roped in' as he said, to use his voice in radio advertising.

Rehearsing a couple of advertising 'spots' at the Voice of Kenya studios one evening, everything seemed to go wrong.   Charles was heard to say, "don't worry chaps, it will VOK on the night."

When television arrived in Kenya, Charles ran his own weekly half-hour program, '*Talking Point*', in which he interviewed 'interesting' people. One of the most amusing moments took place during an interview with Doctor Njorogi Mungai, known as the 'most handsome African in Kenya'.

"Do you smoke?" asked Charles.

"A little," answered Mungai.

"Do you drink?" said Charles.

"A little," answered Mungai.

"Are you married, Doctor Mungai?" asked Charles.

There was a second's pause before Mungai answered, smiling slowly and enigmatically, "A little."

Another interview on this popular television program was with Malin Sorsbie, (who was later knighted, giving his name to a Nairobi art gallery).

In 1946, he had been Captain Malin Sorsbie, General Manager for East African Airways, when there were only four light aircraft belonging to the company. By 1948, 25 more planes had been added.

Now, in the mid-50's, holding a position with Kenya's Wild Life Conservation Program, Sorsbie was put 'rather on the spot' during the television show, '*Talking Point*,' when Charles asked several evocative questions ending with why were there so few Africans introduced into Sorsbie's programs?

There was a little blustering and a few unanswered questions. After the show, Malin Sorsbie's wife stalked after Charles shouting "you baaastard!" in her high-pitched American accent.

It was then Charles' turn to smile enigmatically.

One of Charles' most interesting discussions, he agreed, was held in a later interview with visiting world-known historian, Marjory Perham, who had the reputation of being a formidable six-foot tall Oxford female don -- as they were called.

At that time, nearing her 70's, Marjory Perham, who had devoted her career to studying British colonial administration, talked about a seminar she had conducted at Oxford's Nuffield on African nationalism. Her grand theme was 'colonial responsibility'. Fiercely critical of British rule, she was then the scourge of the colonial office. Always intellectually curious, Charles talked to her about her substantial two-volume biography on Lord Lugard, whose name is indelibly associated with British indirect rule in Africa.

Charles said later, "I think I can say, quite truthfully, that we both enjoyed a tremendously interesting discussion."

For this interview Charles received letters of congratulations from the program controllers at Kenya Broadcasting Corporation;

"I felt I must write you a short note to congratulate you on the absolutely first class discussions last night with Marjory Perham. I thought your technique, and in fact everything connected to the program, had a finesse which I have rarely seen better anywhere."
                                                        Robert. KBC.

Another letter followed from Tony Dean, KBS, which read:

"Just a short line to thank you most warmly on your ready co-operation on the Marjory Perham program and the splendid part you played in it. It was first class in every way and I do sincerely thank you for making possible perhaps the best piece of television which has yet gone out in Kenya."

In 1956, while on safari together in the Mount Kenya area, Charles and his friend District Commissioner Terence Gavaghan heard that a large house facing the mountain was for sale. Charles and Terence went to look at the place. "God knows what we would have done with it, had we even considered buying the house, but we were curious," said Charles.

"Just as we were setting off home, having 'cased' the whole property, a huge storm swept up over the mountain. Sensibly we decided to stay overnight, but the only room ready for guests, smiled the caretaker slyly, was the Bridal Suite, which made for a lot of laughs by our friends when, later, it was found out that Terence and I had stayed there.

"But there were two beds in that room," Charles insisted.

Eventually, Nairobi hotelier Jack Block bought the mansion, then known as Mawingo ('clouds'), but when actor William Holden was filming in the Mount Kenya area, Jack sold the place to him, renaming the magnificent building, Mount Kenya Safari Club."

It was rumoured that Holden's silent business partner was Sir Winston Churchill.

At the end of 1957, Archbishop Makarios, (Primate of the Orthodox Church of Cyprus), arrived in Nairobi from Cyprus, where there was a very unpleasant British-Cyprus situation.

"I visited Makarios each morning at his suite in Nairobi's Norfolk Hotel," said Charles, who was, as always, looking for discussion, with the possibility of top news and pictures.

"One morning I walked into the hotel, Roliflex camera ready to roll, to see, with amazement, a visiting British member of Parliament kneeling at Makarios's feet and kissing the ring on the Archbishop's finger. With hardly a second's hesitation I pointed my camera at this incredible scene, pressed the button, then rushed off and had the film processed immediately and sent to London. Britons, at that time, were being killed in Cyprus, so my timely picture of this moment was of utmost importance. Next day it appeared in every English newspaper. In those days photographs published in the overseas press would be worth about two UK pounds. This one brought in 1,000 UK pounds."

One of the most popular night time, mid-60's radio advertising programs in Kenya, was '*Night Beat*', (for Schweppes). At midnight every night for a contracted few weeks, Charles would play romantic recordings such as Ella Fitzgerald singing, 'What is this Thing Called Love' or Cleo Laine's, 'I've Got you Under My Skin'. Louis Armstrong, singing in his sexy, gravely voice, 'What a Wonderful World', was a *Night Beat* winner, and Charles sometimes ended the program with Peggy Lee singing, 'Nice Girls Don't Stay for Breakfast'. Often the subtle, dulcimer sounds of George Shearing's orchestra could be heard between the liquid gluck-gluck of a Scotch, (for instance), being poured, followed by Schweppes soda water fizzing into a glass.

One night Charles, adding to his program, told listeners that when he had met and talked to Louis Armstrong in Nairobi, he asked him what he did when he was not singing.

"Everything you do, Charles -- but more often!" came the lightening-quick reply.[13]

Sir Roy H. Thomson, (of Fleet), born in Toronto, Canada, was interested in the *Nation* newspaper's technology and enjoyed assisting with interviews. He also believed in Charles' principles to train Africans in journalism with an end to finding managerial positions for them.

During the occasions Sir Roy visited Kenya, some of the *Nation* staff would join him for lunch on Wednesdays.

"There he would sit, smiling at the new comic books surrounding him and reading out jokes that made his thick, bottle-bottom spectacle lens steam up as he laughed.

"On one of his later visits, in 1965, I suggested that Sir Roy should meet the famous Polish artist, Feliks Topolski, who was visiting East Africa for BBC, especially to sketch a series of pictures of Jomo Kenyatta.

"With Feliks standing behind me, well within hearing distance and waiting to be introduced, Sir Roy snarled loudly in his Canadian accent, 'Never heard of the guy.'

Feliks was embarrassed and rather taken aback, as I was. He never forgot the snub. Later, when a party of us took Feliks on safari to Treetops, he sketched some amazing pictures of the baboons that ran about all over the place. To our amusement, when he showed us the pictures, every baboon had Sir Roy's face!"

The next time Topolski visited Kenya, Charles wrote a full-page feature of his work, headlined '*Topolski's View of Kenya*', by-lined, '*The man who watched and recorded history in the making*'. It appeared in

---

[13] Louis Armstrong, who died in 1970 at age 70, changed the world of popular sound in the history of music.

the *Sunday Nation* which also featured many of the sketches the artist had done while in Kenya:

"ON THE FRINGE of the big events of 1961, in Kenya a man stood quietly, watching, saying nary a word, part of the scene, but himself unseen. He had the faculty of merging into the crowds he watched, so that he caught the excitement of their mood and, unobtrusively, he translated that mood through his flying crayons on to sketchpads.

This was Feliks Topolski, artist at large, one of the most dynamic figures of his craft. He recorded history-in-the-making at a critical time of Kenya's constitutional development.

Part of the John Freeman U.S. 'Face to Face' team, which had come to Kenya to interview Jomo Kenyatta, Topolski was noting changes round him from the country he had first known in 1944. Then, as an official British war artist, he visited Polish refugee camps set up in Kenya for those who fled the Russian advances in Eastern Europe. The work he did in those days can still be seen in the Imperial War Museum, London -- pictures of stark misery, of relief, of hope, of endeavour, among a distraught population from which he himself had sprung.

His bitingly satirical brush travelled the post-war world, but never mockingly. More deeply than a camera, his portraits hewed out the tensions and emotions of men and women whom he saw as they built their new lives in the bustling, ebullient times when freedom was on the anvil.

So, too, he looked at Kenya -- at its deeply emotional political meetings, at the man who was destined to become Kenya's first President, at the companions who surrounded him -- and his sketchpads gave those times immorality.

Today, at 57, Topolski publishes -- from his studio under the railway line at Hungerford Bridge, London -- his books of sketches more graphic than words could have captured. And quietly, without bias, he lets the world know how they looked when it was busy with the living and he was quiet with his watching."

With his East African Press Exchange working well, Charles signed the company up as the Kenya centre for *Agence France Presse (AFP)* news service, with coverage in non-British countries and the world; offering better coverage for African countries than did Reuters.

"There was an embarrassing evening though," admitted Charles. "After signing up with AFP, I organised a drinks party for many of my media friends; Henry Reuter, Jack Ensoll, Alistair Mattheson, Anthony Lavers, editors of all the magazines and newspapers (not many at that time), and all radio media to witness the first incoming dispatch of the English AFP service of East Africa. We waited and waited, cocktails in hand, for the latest news to come through on a 'ticker tape'.

"At 8pm the machine started up. With bated breath we all looked for the top news to arrive. To my horror, and to the greatest amusement of my guests, the whole lot came out in French! It took some time to live that down.

"At that point we lost all prospective customers. Nevertheless we stayed with AFP."

Charles was a 'stringer', (news correspondent), for the English newspapers, *Daily Mail* and the *News Chronicle,* and gave regular news broadcasts for BBC, (The British Broadcasting Corporation, Foreign Service), anchoring talk shows during the early days of Kenya television and later, news 'spots' for the American Broadcasting Company.

He also launched *Taifa*, meaning *The Nation*, a daily newspaper in the Kiswahili language in which many Kenyan writers were given the chance to write freely about the drive towards independence and which he hoped would help raise standards in the name-calling, scurrilous Nairobi newspaper scene of the time.

From the first day of publication, the masthead of *Taifa* was a statement of intent. "But in the unruly conditions of 1958," Charles commented, "the project of publishing in a vernacular language was a leap in the dark. Nevertheless, *Taifa* was attracting readers."

Dr. Njorogi Mungai. Interviewed by Charles on Kenya Television's "Talking Point".

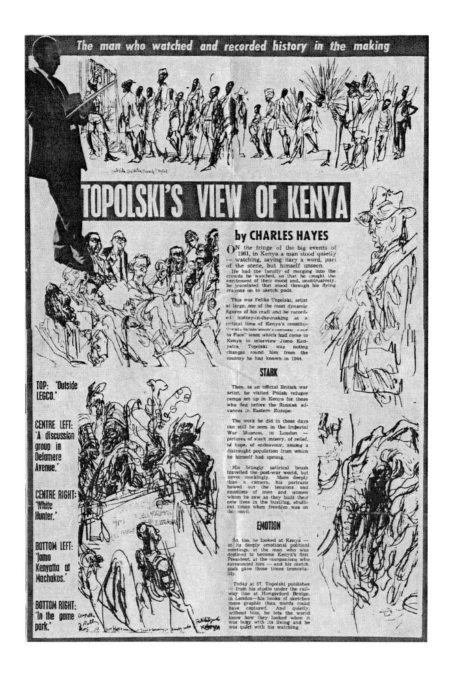

The man who watched and recorded history in the making

TOPOLSKI'S VIEW OF KENYA

by CHARLES HAYES

ON the fringe of the big events of 1961, in Kenya a man stood quietly watching, saying nary a word, part of the scene, but himself unseen.

He had the faculty of merging into the crowds he watched, so that he caught the excitement of their mood and, unobtrusively, he translated that mood through his flying crayons on to sketch pads.

This was Feliks Topolski, artist at large, one of the most dynamic figures of his craft and he recorded history-in-the-making at a critical time of Kenya's constitutional development. A member of the BBC's Face to Face team which had come to Kenya to interview Jomo Kenyatta, Topolski was noting changes round him from the country he had known in 1944.

STARK

Then, as an official British war artist, he visited Polish refugee camps set up in Kenya for those who fled before the Russian advances in Eastern Europe.

The work he did in those days can still be seen in the Imperial War Museum, in London — pictures of stark misery, of relief, of hope, of endeavour, among a distraught population from which he himself had sprung.

His bitingly satirical brush travelled the post-war world, but never mockingly. More deeply than a camera, his portraits hewed out the tensions and emotions of men and women whom he saw as they built their new lives in the bustling, ebullient times when freedom was on the anvil.

EMOTION

So, too, he looked at Kenya — at its deeply emotional political meetings, at the man who was destined to become Kenya's first President, at the companions who surrounded him — and his sketch pads gave those times immortality.

Today at 57, Topolski publishes — from his studio under the railway line at Hungerford Bridge, in London—his books of sketches more graphic than words could have captured. And quietly, without bias, he lets the world know how they looked when it was busy with its living and he was quiet with his watching.

TOP: 'Outside LEGCO.'

CENTRE LEFT: 'A discussion group in Delamere Avenue.'

CENTRE RIGHT: 'White Hunter.'

BOTTOM LEFT: 'Jomo Kenyatta at Machakos.'

BOTTOM RIGHT: 'In the game park.'

FIFTEEN

PARTNERSHIP

"Without a (news) paper or journal,
you cannot combine a community."
Ghandi

IN 1958, CHARLES MET Michael Curtis, the youngest editor in Fleet Street.

When Michael left England's *News Chronicle*, following a row with the ownership over Britain's Suez invasion, which he opposed, the newspaper was already in trouble.

Leaving well before the newspaper closed, Michael was snapped up quickly as personal aide to the young Aga Khan, to join him on a journey during which His Highness was to meet the East African Ismaili community.

Charles recalled, "*Taifa* covered those events and at press conferences Michael and I chatted. In his quiet way this Fleet Street legend enquired about *Taifa*'s editorial policy and the stories it was carrying.

"Somehow the conversation took us into Nairobi's Equator Club. At 3a.m. that morning, with the band still playing softly, Michael Curtis said he would like to join the *Taifa* venture.

"He outlined the idea that in making *Taifa* into East Africa's best Swahili newspaper, we could also expect to hive off an English language paper which he would edit. 'Just translate some of those stories you're printing and, in English, they would be winners,' he said. He also laid down the dictum that we must write ourselves out of jobs and from the

Michael Curtis and Charles Hayes look on as His Highness the Aga Khan
examines a company result chart in the *Nation* offices, Nairobi.
(pic: *Daily Nation*)

beginning we must train African editors and managers to take over, say, in 10 years time.

"At the time none of us realized that we were being approached, through Michael, by the Aga Khan. Thus, when it was suggested that I find a means of printing our own newspaper, I located a small, Asian (East Indian)-owned jobbing printer in the back streets of Nairobi who had a sheet-fed press. It looked like a cheap solution and when Curtis returned to East Africa he came to inspect my selection.

"In his friendly way he said, 'Charles, I think we can do better than that.' Then he divulged that his proposals were being financed by His Highness the young Aga Khan and that the target was a newspaper group to cover the whole of East Africa."

Back in 1937, H.H. the Aga Khan senior, and his wife the Begum Aga Khan, visited Kenya where he was weighed and presented with his weight in gold by his many Ismaili followers. The Aga Khan senior thanked the Ismaili Khojas graciously for the gold, but asked them to receive it back for the benefit and uplift of the community.

It was only the second time the Aga Khan had been weighed in gold -- the first time in Bombay, India on 19th January 1936, on the occasion of his Golden Jubilee.

Charles could see clearly his earlier dream coming true.

" *East African Newspapers (Nation Series) Ltd.*, was born on April 1st, 1959, with Michael Curtis as Managing Director and *Taifa* its only publication, a tabloid. I introduced Dr. B Mareka Gecaga to Michael who asked him to be our first African Director, which he accepted. The former Press Exchange was a shareholder and the new company appointed Mrs. (Althea) Tebbutt as its advertising Director. I became the first Editorial Director."[14]

---

[14] While a *Nation Group* Director, Charles founded the *East African Guild of Editors* and was selected by Zurich's International Press Institute to 'blueprint' and set up two schools of journalism, to provide

A printing expert from Britain arrived to dazzle the new company with explanations of the offset litho printing method which was taking the newspaper world by storm.

"An offset plant was ordered, the first of its kind in East Africa, although typesetting was, initially, to be carried out on the old 'hot lead' Linotype machines we had acquired. We moved from our small Victoria Street premises further up the road into what became known as *Nation House*.

"In those days Michael was often away recruiting journalists, checking on the printing plant revolution, listening to developments, ordering the latest photo-setting device to give us higher quality results than East Africa had ever seen. Finally a print works in Nairobi's Industrial Area was acquired and soon, in March 1960, the *Sunday Nation* was launched with experienced London journalists producing it. This situation meant that perfectly truthful statements became disturbing to some groups.

"For instance, soon after his release by the colonial authorities, Jomo Kenyatta paid me a visit. He was not pleased at what we were publishing. Kenyatta was an old friend of mine, but on that day he had a grouch. 'You are too sensational, Cha-less,' he told me gruffly. (Having spent years in Britain he seemed to regard tabloids with the same distaste as do many Britons themselves). Despite anything I could say in defense of the *Nation* brand of journalism, he wasn't pleased. And I wasn't prepared to give an inch. For all our differences of opinions, Jomo Kenyatta and I remained good friends.

"At Nairobi's Government House the Nation Group was also looked on with disfavour. A close relative of the Governor told me that in those grand halls we were called, 'The Daily Filthy' (I was somewhat mollified when she told me the *East African Standard*, the only other

---

training for African newcomers into the press business, to teach responsible journalism and to hold on to the Freedom of the Press.

English daily, was known as the Two-Minute Silence, for she said, 'that's how long it takes to read.'

"Our Swahili newspaper, *Taifa Leo, (Nation Today)*, soon became a well-read daily and six months after publishing the *Sunday Nation* came the *Daily Nation*, launched at a most critical point in Kenya's political history. Transportation experts mapped out distribution runs east and west of Nairobi and soon we were delivering by air to Tanzania and Uganda."

As Editorial Director of East African Newspapers (Nation group) Ltd., Charles was, at last, in his element.

Amongst the many articles Charles was writing at this time there was a special piece for the Information Department magazine, *Kenya Today*.

Headlined 'Carnival at Baragoi', he wrote about people of the Samburu tribe, showing how they had moved towards a better life when they built a hospital for themselves in the rugged part of Kenya where they lived:

"THE SAMBURU tribesmen, who live in the arid little trading centre at Baragoi, south of Lake Rudolph, (also known as 'the Jade Sea'), have until now only seen the White man's medicine in the form of a travelling dispensary -- a camel carrying drugs and two medical orderlies walking alongside it.

It was a great occasion when the new hospital was opened to the primitive Samburu, whose whole life is centred around the herds of cattle and their grazing. A permanent building, to the nomads of this remote and rugged part of Kenya, is almost as unusual as a day of steady rain. On the day of the opening ceremony, tribesmen began at dawn to start moving into Baragoi from their scattered, mud-walled manyattas (houses). Money, eighteen thousand shining shillings, had been collected through the sale of Samburu and Turkana stock. Stones for the hospital had been hewn by hand. And when eventually opening day arrived, the 2000 elders, chiefs and warriors, waiting patiently in the searing sunshine, stirred proudly. Meanwhile, in the "High Street" of dusty Baragoi, with its four shops, the women -- by custom not allowed at men's gatherings -- were buying treasures which the proceeds of cattle-sales provided for them.

Suddenly, as their young District Officer walked amongst them, they surrounded him, dancing and singing in their rhythmic, tuneless way.

To show their respect for him they followed ancient custom and spat at him!

Opening of Baragoi Hospital 1955. District Commissioner Terence Gavaghan (leaning against pole) (pic: *Tazama Magazine*)

In the cool of evening, at a river camp under the great thorn trees, District Commissioner Terry Gavaghan thought over the day. 'Normally, peaceful administration is intolerably boring to Africans,' mused Gavaghan, "we have done away with the excitement and the fun of the past, but an occasion like this gives them something to be proud of.' The village down the road bore the testimony for this view, as the Baragoi women danced their way into their new medical future."

Jean and Charles Hayes' had bought a coffee shamba, (farm), named Willowhayne, in Kiambu, on the outskirts of Nairobi. And it was from that 'great barn of a house', with its large, overgrown garden, that Charles organised several BBC interviews.

One important one was with Jomo Kenyatta, after Kenyatta's release from detention. Carefully, Charles organised the BBC film and sound crew who waited nervously for Kenyatta to arrive.

Late, but ready to talk to Charles, Kenyatta, prodding a seedy-looking flower bed with his amber-topped walking stick, looked at the garden, then at the house said, with a gruff voice,

"This is a terrible place Cha-less, it looks like an African squatter's camp. I'm not doing an interview here."

And with a flourish of his beaded flywhisk he called for his big black car and took off with the driver.

"It took me most of the afternoon to track him down, but I found Jomo Kenyatta at last in Lavarini's, his favourite Italian restaurant on Government road, Nairobi, where he greeted me with a belly laugh.

We did the interview next morning sitting in Sir Derek and Lady Erskin's beautiful, flower-bordered gardens in Riverside Drive, Nairobi.

Later, when Charles visited Kenyatta in his house in Gatundu, Kenyatta reminisced about the story Charles had written about him, (for the *Daily Nation*), while he had been detained in Lodwa, 'far from civilisation,' Kenyatta commented wryly. Charles had been on leave in

England and had visited the English pubs in west Sussex, where Jomo Kenyatta had been a 'regular' during World War II. He talked to the many people with whom Kenyatta had worked and made friends. Said one woman, "he used to come down to the White Horse Pub on his bicycle, but never drank more than two pints of bitter before cycling home. 'Jambo', as we called him, was a thorough gentleman who conducted himself quietly. He always wore blue shorts at weekends, winter and summer. He had lovely strong limbs."

Another person remembered him shopping with his English wife on Saturday mornings, and at other times when walking alone on The Downs.

"The Germans can do what they will, but they can't get rid of The Sussex Downs," chuckled Kenyatta after an enjoyable evening stroll there during the war.

In 'The Half Moon and Anchor Inn pubs, all the 'regulars' remembered that the bearded 'Jambo' had several gold teeth, wore a ring with a cornelian stone and worked at a mushroom and flower farm.

"He was never a work dodger and was very strong. On occasion he would take on heavier jobs than he should have, at his age."

There was nothing wrong with knowing 'Jambo', said his friends, underlining that he was 'a very good chap' and they didn't believe what the rest of the world was saying about him, but wished him luck

"This is his opportunity to get to the top," they said, hoping he would come back to see them some day so that the pub owner could serve him another 'bitter' or two.

Kenyatta had read Charles' story at that time, but now asked about 'Bill', one pub owner, and the health of some of the other men he knew.

After a few emotional moments, he said, quietly, "You got it right, Cha-less."

One year a film company arrived in Kenya to shoot a film with the working title '*Safari*'. Over 100 Africans were to take part in the production as "Mau Mau" terrorists, thirty African askaris (guards) and Charles, as a part–time, known talented actor, was asked to take the part of a Kenyan police officer.

"It was an amusing few weeks," said Charles, who spent many hours with the main characters of the film, Victor Mature, (called Victor 'Manure' by film staff), and Janet Leigh. Another film followed named "Mogambo", when Charles was asked to play the part of Dirk Bogart's brother.

Over the years many films were shot in Kenya and most times Charles was offered parts in them which he accepted

Thinking over some of the events in his life that had amused him, Charles remembered the time he was covering a ceremony for the newspaper where the Governor of Kenya, Sir Phillip Mitchell, decked out in his white Colonial finery and large feather-plumed hat was holding forth to the thousands of Africans who were watching his every move. Charles' African assistant, looking very puzzled indeed, asked, "Why is the Governor wearing a kuku (chicken) on his head?"

"There were always times to laugh, even at life's worst moments," chuckled Charles.

"For instance one early morning a bus driver, overtired after travelling through the night from an up-country township into the city of Nairobi, missed the large round-about in the main road. Half asleep he drove over it, smashing through the fence of a large hotel. The bus, full of sleepy women and children, landed in the swim pool-- a perfect fit.

"When the bus crashed into the pool it caused all the water to splash out onto the lawns like a tidal wave, enabling passengers to climb to safety. Large bunches of bananas and chickens squawking in their cages were still firmly attached to the bus roof. A huge loudspeaker teetered on the outside front of the bus and, probably because of the sudden jolt, began to play extremely loud music."

While trying to piece together the events that had led up to the accident, Charles asked an African onlooker what had happened.

"Si Jui (I don't know)," answered the man, shrugging his shoulders, "but what a silly place to put a swimming pool."

The headmaster of the Duke of York School, in Nairobi, asked Charles if he would come to talk to his English-class students about newspaper, television and magazine reporting. Delighted to discuss his favourite subject, especially to youngsters who, he hoped, would become the talented writers Kenya would need, Charles visited the school, spending an afternoon with the bright, interested group.

He talked about 'A Word' and its power of happiness or destruction; the combination of words which someone can weave into poetry, or strong emotional appeal. He continued, with much discussion, about the communications of words -- the word of mouth in tribal councils, the word which spelt death, and war and love.

He went on to talk of the coming of printing, with the large, solid type letters and the printing of books; bestseller bibles; the lampoons and tracts of Fleet Street; the magazine, which was the small book, and the *Telegraph* and the man who had put his printing press aboard a ferry boat so that he could compete with news -- and gain customers.

The build-up of the great newspapers -- *The Times*, of England, founded more than a century and a half ago-- still going strong --and the death of newspapers, and he discussed the duties and responsibilities of anyone who controls the means of communications between people and people.

"What we want to examine today," Charles continued, "is the organised institution of the Press, this mass medium of communication of words and ideas, this public service to which writers devote their lives, sometimes fanatically, this overworked, underpaid, under-recognised, under-praised, over-glamorised profession to which I belong.

"So what is it all about, this medium into which men have poured millions of their money in the free countries -- and have struggled to control elsewhere. Is it the percentage of sex that he puts in his pages? In some cases yes -- and this is even truer of women's magazines. But your newspapers try to carry news, information for people about people and the events they are creating. But what kind of news? 'If it bleeds it leads' usually grabs readership attention, but you can break the thing right down by a study of news content of the British newspapers -- for instance, in *The Times* and the *Guardian*, you'll find that factual news makes up 35 per cent of the paper; in *The Mirror*, human interest -- and when I say human, I mean ......" (There was great laughter here by the students).

Charles went on, "Human interest stories in *The Mirror* far outweigh anything political which is taking place in countries and their parliaments.

"Between 40 and 50 per cent of a paper is made up of advertising -- and this in itself is a service, both to readers who want to hear of new products on the markets and to the manufacturers who want to sell their products and, let's face it, a newspaper without advertising is like winking at a girl in the dark, so how much does the editor, then, pay attention to these two facets of his trade -- his reading public and the advertisers.

"Is he leading the one along by the nose and the other by the moneybags?

"I have kept the conversation away from Kenya long enough. When you talk of Britain, you can see clear recognizable patterns of behaviour, but in Kenya, heaven preserve us. Here the job of writing news is simple, you would say; we have a number of different peoples, trying to become a nation. They grind different axes which they swing at the heads of people but especially at the Press.

"Today, a Minister of Parliament had some harsh words to say about the Press. It is a statement he made today in Paris -- a city to which he was attracted by the chance of making a speech -- about the Press. He expects now to be reported by the Press, which he attacks. He will be -- because that's the way the darn thing works -- a sort of masochistic 'beat me, Daddy' complex called 'freedom'.

"In Kenya, in the newspaper offices of Kenya, men slide round the doors with their statements of view. The postbags are full of them; there are hundreds of them a day -- and if they do not get published, there is dismay and discontent and then the charges that 'this or that paper is against us.'

"Regularly, in the *Nation Series*, we have both parties saying to us that we favour the other side. But the violent reactions have included hints that these men will do everything they can to control the press in the future. Only the other day a minister of the present government commented: 'The only free press that should be out here is the freedom to publish handouts from the government.'

"Is that to be the future? Will you have a single strong government party in this country which will kill news of criticism? Many countries of the world would agree with nationalist leaders here that a country is happier if it has no conflict of thoughts.

"A Director of the International Press Institute came through Nairobi a little while ago. I met him at the airport and asked him which country he was going on to. He said, 'Indonesia, where we have three editors just about to be hanged.'

"Editors have been in the forefront of many of the national fights in the world and they have been engulfed in rebellions. And life is cheap. Journalists get flung into jail. They write about it afterwards, but a jail is a jail is a jail -- and the floors are cold and the beds are hard. The fact is that newspapers have one great job to do -- to help that process of human liberation -- to remove the shackles which stop a man questioning what his government does and asking his friends whether or not the policy of the country's government is right or wrong.

"Men are growing in capacity to govern and with the power to reason -- that is the process which newspapermen want to encourage; the faculty of criticism, the impersonal examination of an idea by men who have knowledge, or who want knowledge. The right of a man to reply to criticism, the right of a man to say what he has seen -- these are the inbuilt freedoms which are ours in the western democracies.

"There must be the right to suggest alternatives, but the only chance of the Press in Kenya, and in east Africa generally, is that the people will demand that right...

"I hope, that in our task of nation building, we shall have you -- all of you -- with us, and that we can write into the constitution that one phrase: The freedom of the press is guaranteed."

TAZAMA

THE MAGAZINE FOR AFRICANS

Published by East African Standard Ltd
on behalf of
The East Africa High Commission

1952

SIXTEEN

New Friends, Unusual Safaris

"Africa always has something new to offer."
Pliny, A.D.23-79

IN 1958, CHARLES MET Canadian doctor Edward Margetts and his wife, Margo, who would remain friends for the rest of his life.

In up-country Kenya, in the hills of Kisii, in the province of South Nyanza, approximately 350 miles from Nairobi, there is a village well known not only for its unique pink, white and grey soap-stone, from which hand-carved figures and African animals are made and sold, but where local witchdoctors, masters of the ancient art of 'trepanning', (opening the scalp), operate.

For centuries Kisii witchdoctors have had great success with the trepanning operation. Now Charles was ready to see this operation for himself, knowing also that an interesting story was there for the writing.

Having made plans, and obtained permission, to attend a Kisii tribal trepanning operation, Charles, armed with camera and notebook, arrived in the small up-country African village.

Doctor John Grounds, the Government Medical Officer from Kisii hospital, accompanied him. The other Doctor very excited to observe the operation was Ted Margetts, the Canadian psychiatrist in charge of Nairobi's Mathari Mental Hospital (1955 to'59), who had studied this rare but centuries-old form of surgery.

"It was an incredible experience," said Charles. "Before the trepanning on a young girls' head began, she was given a potent drink to ease any pain the operation might cause.

"Pieces of hammered metal were used as primitive surgeon's knives, to cut carefully through the layers of skin on her scalp. Water for swilling away blood came straight from the river and was poured from a wide, green, plastic bowl held under the patient's chin. The witchdoctor said his operations were always successful; all headaches he dealt with in this way were cured.

"After the operation, which took about two hours, the girl walked away looking a bit dazed, but otherwise in good spirits. Small bone chips had been removed from her scalp and her headache had gone. It turned out that a few days before the operation she had bumped her head badly on a low door- post."

Summing up the whole operation, Charles said, "Frankly, I think an aspirin or two might have been an easier method of easing her pain."

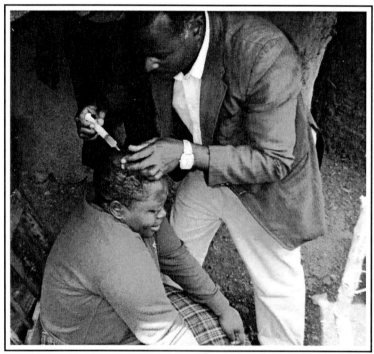

A trepanning operation in Kisii highlands, Kenya (pic: E. Margetts)

By evening Charles and Margetts had formed a friendship. Charles had a story and Ted had enough information to write a paper that was presented, a few years later, at a United Medical Conference in Madrid.

They arranged, then, to get permission to attend another interesting meeting; a Maasai Eunoto Ceremony, (the coming of age of Maasai boys and the selection of a chief), they had heard was due to happen sometime soon in another part of Kenya.

"That safari turned out to last several days with a lot of running up and down rolling Maasai country," said Charles, who later wrote the story of their safari, and the meaning of eunoto, which was published in the August, 1958 issue of *Kenya Weekly News*, with the title;

'The Significance of the Eunoto Ceremony: We the Wealthy Ones. Riddle of the Maasai.'

Here are some excerpts:

"ONE DAY, someone with the requisite knowledge will have the leisure to make a definitive, up-to-date assessment of the riddle of the Kenya Maasai and how much social change is weaving itself into their insular way of life; that pattern which made them masters of Kenya last century.

The colour and observance of complex tradition in this month's eunoto ceremony seems merely to stress that Sir Claude Hollis' book, outlining the custom in 1905, is entirely applicable today.

From the basis of a life which was fashioned centuries ago the Maasai have made perfunctory examination of the progress for which other African peoples clamour -- education, preventative medicine, access to better diet, more wealth -- and rejected it.

Why? The Maasai do not give a better reason than that they consider Western civilization values all wrong. Secretly, many Britons admire them for it!

More than half a century ago a Governor of Kenya, Sir Charles Elliot, writing of the Maasai, stated gloomily: "The future of these people is not an easy problem. They resemble the lion and the leopard, strong and beautiful beasts of prey, that please the artistic sense, but are never any use and often a serious danger.

"Even so," Sir Charles went on, "the manly virtues, fine earrings and often handsome features of the Maasai arouse a certain sympathy but it can hardly be denied that they have hitherto done no good in this world that anyone knows of."

But, was he right?

The story is told of a recent traveller in Maasailand who found himself unable to converse with the people. Kiswahili and English brought no response and, skittishly, he greeted those he met in French and German.

From a Maasai, wearing just a blanket, holding a spear in his hand, standing tall and red-ochred, he was startled to hear a reply in perfect German. He was talking to a tribesman who had studied and worked in Berlin for 16 years -- who had thrown away his city life of comparative ease, though stressful, in order to return to the one he considered happier and more satisfying.

Thus it is that the Eunoto ceremony, taking place in Maasailand, deserves attention and in the New Africa, so rapidly becoming drab and seriously parochial, provides exciting contact with the old, however outmoded that may seem to be.

This traditional method of qualifying through warriorhood, for the part of the governance of the tribal affairs, is probably as ancient as the tribe itself. Eunoto, according to Hollis, means 'the selection of the chief.' Certainly the idea provides a central theme for the ceremony.

But the drama underlying is the fact that, week-long feast over, the warrior-grade, (il moran), have almost completed their period of 'national service' and have taken the first step towards accepting responsibility as junior elders of the tribe. It is progress which, even today, is unwanted and unpopular. Traditionally, therefore, the carefree moran have marked this transition into serious life by preceding it with some months of meat-feasts and love -- to get in the mood perhaps.

Weeks ago a medicine man decided on the place where a new, immaculate manyatta (group of housing) was to be built. The site, free from bad magic and conducive to good luck, was on the Uaso Kedong River, some 20 miles off the Rift Valley Escarpment highway. Last month, mothers of the warriors built the characteristic low, flat-topped, (mud and cow dung) houses in a wide ellipse, after elders had lit a fire in a log in the centre of this space.

As the new moon was sighted, the ceremony began. At dawn the following morning the warriors prayed, standing still as glistening statues, a dramatic frieze from another century.

Red ochre was mixed with sheep fat and carefully rubbed into the muscle-rippled bodies of the moran. Liquid and gaudy, the ochre and fat was teased through their long, braided hair. Lion mane headdresses, bead necklaces in favoured shades and a yard or so of cloth, draped toga-like across one shoulder, completed the garb of the preening Maasai dandies.

No spears or shields were carried, for this is a peaceful ceremony. Everything in the manyatta is bent towards their pleasure; the few mothers attending the ceremony, mothers of the warriors with a group of young, uncircumcised girls, saw to the warrior's make-up and providing water and firewood, but the main requirement was that there should be sufficient milk and meat. In forest glades and away from women, (who must not look upon the meat lest it be contaminated by their presence), 49 cattle were slaughtered this first day in order to satisfy the warriors -- in the ratio of one beast to ten men.

When the sun was high, a kudu war-horn shrieked out its urgent notes; the moran came running to the quarter-mile-wide arena formed by the huts. Singing and loping through the melee in happy, mock-battle groups, bouncing high into the air as easily as rubber balls, one felt the crackling electricity of the moment as these hardy people gave free range to their joy of living and danced on into the glowing evening.

The second day belonged to the elders. In groups, the moran were taken to the forests on nearby hills and were reminded of the long, proud history of the Maasai, the responsibilities they would assume in the future.

The elders had made their selection of a warrior who would henceforth lead the age-grade. He was required to be beautiful in the body, of unblemished parentage; he must not have killed anyone, must be wise and calculating, for his orders will be obeyed implicitly by the members of the age-grade from now on.

The unhappy youth was then seized and told of his selection as leader; the nomination had been kept secret from the moran until this moment for the post is unpopular. Had they been warned, most of the warriors would have taken steps immediately to defile their characters, rather than be chosen as leader.

From that moment on, the ol ononi, (as a new leader is called), was a man apart, separated from the comradeship which had become part of his life in the republic of the young men. He now leads the ancient ceremonial and he it was whose head was first shorn of the prized, free-swinging hair on the third day of the ceremony. His companions followed, by area sectors, shivering with rage and mortification as their mothers shaved heads in the early morning sunlight. There must always be other warriors and the young endito -- girls aged from 11 to 13 -- watching during this miserable half hour.

During the morning, a newly bald moran was selected to slaughter a bullock, plunging the knife into the nape of its neck. The meat is for the mothers and represents the gift which compensates them for a loss; they will never again be called 'Mother' by these lusty sons.

On the fifth day, when the warrior's heads were completely shaven, elders led them to a secret place in the hills, miles from the manyatta. From early morning the long file of brown bodies climbed, (with Doctor Margetts and myself following), over the loose volcanic rock which makes up the skirt of Mount Suswa. Where they moved through the wispy grass, it became red with the ochre brushed off their legs. Finally, silent and awed, they entered an enclave and posted sentries on the high rocks which surrounded it.

A white-necked, black bullock was slaughtered and its heart and lungs carefully removed.

Noiselessly the warriors filed into a circle marked by an elder carrying the heart, with which three times he touched the forehead and nose of each warrior. Two bites of the raw meat were allowed each man, strong teeth grabbing at the symbol of strength. Another elder slipped on the right-hand middle finger of each youth a sliver of skin from another bullock. In the open, there was the silence of an empty church, for this was the moment of manhood.

Darkness fell. The elders now disclosed to the moran the name chosen for their age-grade, pace setter for the whole of Kenya Maasailand. The Ilaitete, they would be called – 'Those Who Have Wealth.'

Delighted, the warriors scrambled down the hillside in the moonlight, leaping happily over the rocky obstacles and singing: Anga, anga, kira Ilaitete -- 'we come, the wealthy ones.'

At the manyatta, as their song rang nearer in the forest, the mothers proud, yet near to tears, chattered in a twitter of excitement and sang prayers to the God in the Sky.

Some, the un-wicked amongst the warriors, those who had not been known to sleep with circumcised girls, were chosen to spend that night in the small singira -- a coveted exclusive club honour. For the others, the night was lost in festivity.

Over the next six months the moran will grow their hair again, will select a bride for their leader and will pay his dowry in cattle -- for until he is married, none of them may take a wife.

In the old days, they would have moved in bands seeking lion to kill and would have been expected to carry out one last terrifying raid.

These days, lion are not plentiful; cattle-rustling is frowned upon and generally means trouble.

Amongst the 500 warriors undergoing eunoto, there were some who spoke a smattering of English sentences, but who quite obviously cared less about this accomplishment than they did for the ochre-designs they drew on their slender limbs made by dragging their fingertips through the thick red ochre spread over their skin.

I sat munching a lettuce salad sandwich, reflecting on all these things. Around me gathered a group of the moran who were at first incredulous, then hilarious and doubled up in helpless laughter as they watched me eat.

They said, 'Leaves to eat? This covered one has the habits of a hare!'

The Maasai diet of milk and meat gave them physical superiority over tribes like the Akikuyu, for instance. Rich in vitamins and high quality protein, the favoured food largely freed the children from the bone deformities, anaemia and dental defects, prevalent amongst their neighbours. But, while cooking and sanitation are not understood, almost all raw meat means tapeworm infestations and a high incidence of conjunctivitis (of the eyes) where water is as scarce as manure is plentiful.

For the Maasai, there is no life better than this.

'It has been this way since we came from the valley,' they comment. They tell of a Maasai over the Tanganyika border who was adjured to sell his cattle and did so. He received thirty thousand English pounds for them, taking the money home with him.

For two weeks he mooned around with the notes. Then he went out and bought some cattle again. Thirty thousand Pounds worth!

But is there anything they want? Yes. If you are going to Maasai country any time, take a handful of sparkling pearly buttons --or a spare shirt to replace that from which you'll be persuaded to rip off the fasteners. Outside of sleek cattle, buttons for wearing in the ears represent just about the only thing attractive for the Maasai moran. No cars, no telephones, no miracle washers and driers.

Mind you, sometimes the news in these crazy days suggests the possibility that the Maasai are right."

While driving back wearily to Nairobi, Dr. Ted Margetts' car, which had carried Charles and himself and an assistant perfectly well to the eunoto ceremony a day or so before, suddenly broke down after an hour into their journey home.

"We were nearing the Kedong River," said Ted. "As it was getting dark, Charles and I decided, we thought wisely, that as it was lion country, and at dusk lions begin to get hungry, we would sleep in the car until morning. But our other passenger absolutely refused to stay in Maasailand one minute longer, so clambering out of the car said that he was going to walk home! Well, we couldn't let him walk so far alone, especially at night where wild animals are known to roam, so Charles and I walked with him, occasionally whistling and talking loudly every time we heard animal noises and twigs cracking around us.

"It took us five, fairly gruelling hours to reach the African village of Kedong where, at almost daylight, we found a local taxi driver who drove us to Nairobi.

"Our night journey over rough terrain, I could see, had been very hard on Charles' legs, but he never complained. We were all ready to lay down on my garden lawn on Whitehouse road which we reached, with relief, at dawn, but my wife Margo, who had been worried sick when we hadn't returned that night as expected, cooked us a tremendous breakfast of eggs and bacon; the best breakfast I ever remembered eating-- and the most exciting safari ever!"

Two old safari buddies, Charles Hayes and Ted Margetts, meet many years later in Steveston, (near Vancouver), in 1995.

Young Maasai take a bite from the still warm bull's heart during their Eunoto ceremony. (pics: E. Margetts)

Maasai form a circle during Eunoto ceremony.
(pic: E. Margetts)

Right: Older tribesmen celebrate with their home-brewed pombe (banana beer)
(pic: CH)

Maasai celebrations. (pic: CH)

SEVENTEEN

A Royal Visit

*"The art of paragraphing is to stroke a platitude
until it purrs like an epigram."*
Don Marquis, 1878-1937

IN FEBRUARY 1959, Charles' BBC weekly *'News Roundup'* contained a report on the visit to Kenya by Her Majesty Queen Elizabeth, the Queen Mother, who had not visited East Africa since 1934.

"THE NEWS about which everyone in Kenya is talking, of course, is the visit of Her Majesty, Queen Elizabeth, the Queen Mother because, in one way or another, it concerns us all. For many people, this is their first opportunity to see a member of the British royal family. For others it is the chance to renew acquaintance with tradition. For others, again, it is the peg on which to hang some politics. But for none of us has life gone along untouched since last Thursday evening when the Queen Mother's aircraft came winging out of a clear Kenya sky and touched down at the airport she was to have opened last year. I think it is true to say that everyone was a little apprehensive because of Kenya's Justice of the Peace, Tom Mboya's decision to boycott the royal event.

The long route from the airport into the City Centre was crowded with people who stood quietly in groups -- with a little worm of anxiety gnawing at them. And then the magic began spreading into the streets.

Thousands of Africans amongst them had been instructed by their political party leaders not to take part in the celebrations. Thousands of others -- members of tribal associations which disagreed with the political leaders' views on the royal visit -- were already in a happy mood as their watches told them that the Queen mother's car would be along the clean-swept streets any moment. And it was almost possible to pick out the societies to which each man belonged. That was before the little procession arrived.

Yet everywhere, as soon as people saw the Queen Mother actually in front of them, the magic took over. Africans who had stood with their hands in their pockets, took them out and gave small uncertain waves and then started cheering a little and the cheers broke into a roar of happiness. For them it must have been a life-giving injection -- something which suddenly awakened formerly faulty body mechanism and gave it life. Faces, which had not smiled for hours, creased into laughter. There was a certain feeling of relief whereas previously there had been only tension. And that is how the visit began.

On Friday, the Queen Mother -- who seems to have the secret of eternal youth -- rested at Government house on Nairobi Hill. But the festooned streets, the huge gold crowns hanging all along Delamere Avenue, the galaxy of massed colour in the new flower beds which have filled formerly empty spaces of dust -- all these reminded us wherever we went that the royal visitor was with us.

On Saturday there took place Nairobi's own festival of youth. From early morning trucks and buses from the schools and outlying areas were full to overflowing with children in the bright colours of their school uniforms. Heightened by the flutter of the diminutive flags they carried, they poured through the streets and on up to the showground arena to take on the appearance of so many thousands of butterflies. On Saturday, too, the garden party to which 7,000 Kenya citizens went in their finest to see and be seen, to talk and to listen, and to let some of the happiness of the occasion rub off on them.

Does all this sound as if something had got into Kenya which was clean and healthful and rejuvenating? Well, that is just the way it seemed to even your hardened newsmen this week. And, as one correspondent of a London newspaper cabled; 'Africans have broken the Mboyacott, repeat Mboyacott.'

And so, until next week, this is Charles Hayes, reporting to you from Nairobi."

Masaai await the Queen Mother's arrival.

Tribal drummers & dancers await the Queen Mother

EIGHTEEN

Talking to the World

"Proper Words in proper places."
Jonathan Swift

THE YEARS LEADING UP to Kenya's Independence, ('Uhuru' - or 'freedom'), in 1963, the newspaper, magazine articles and news broadcasts which took place over that time, and beyond, made indelible entries into the history of east Africa.

Here is a mere cross section of news reportage copies that were written and broadcast by Charles and found within countless files in the year 2000.

For the *Daily Mail* newspaper, London. January 6th, 1960. From Hayes, Nairobi:

"A EUROPEAN SCHOOLBOY – pupil at 'Kenya's Eton', the Prince of Wales school, Nairobi, was jailed for fifteen months as 'ringleader' of a gang of nineteen boys all from the same school, at shop-breaking, attempted robbery and violence, which has shocked Europeans here.

Never before has a European teenager been jailed for theft in this Colony. Nearly all the boys are sons of prominent businessmen and Government officials. In addition to the boy, whose father is a mathematics teacher, two other boys were sentenced today to be caned. Others were probationed."

Radio Roundup 6th August 1960. From Nairobi, Kenya:

"A DIP IN THE BRANTUB OF NEWS this week produces a varied assortment of items alright, and to assess it is probably one of the most difficult weeks we have had in recent months. Here are some samples, taken at random;

Early in the week came a shock at the announcement that an internationally known company manufacturing aluminium products had abandoned its plan for establishing a rolling mill at Mombasa.

If that looked like a debit entry in Kenya's trade books, it was followed almost immediately by more heartening news in agriculture.

From government sources it was learned that tea-growing pilot schemes had been so successful in the Nyambeni Hills and at Ragati that a vast new scheme is now planned which will lead to the planting up of thousands more acres under this valuable crop. The chances are that tea is going to become Kenya's major crop within a few years, and that, in value to African farmers, is going to be better than the money-spinning coffee which has become such a popular planting in recent years.

The whole object of the scheme is to split up the enormous potential of 800-thousand acres of tea-soil between the larger plantation companies and the African smallholder -- spreading the profits enduringly throughout the country's high rainfall areas.

But this news was followed by a demand from the Maasai leaders who want the return of the former Maasai lands, which were opened up at the turn of the century, to make way for modern farming methods.

There has come a spate of bitter invective from some of the Maasai political leaders following advice from the Governor, Sir Patrick Renison, that they get into line with today's political developments and consider themselves and their lands part of a Kenya moving towards independence.

Sir Patrick mentioned - fairly bluntly - that Britain would be unable to guarantee forever the treaty she had made over a century ago with the Maasai.

So this week Maasai leaders came back with the request that if the treaty is to be abrogated, it might as well be broken right now and the lands of which it was a subject should be handed back to the domain of the tribe immediately.

All views are very pertinent at the present time because next week we shall see Kenya undergoing intensive campaigning to register on the new voters' roles being prepared.

Between one and two million Africans will be enfranchised by the end of September, it is thought, and we can expect election fever to hit the place shortly afterwards. We sometimes envy the strong, reassuring statements which come from our neighbour's territory south of Kenya. But there's just a chance that we shall start hearing something similar soon amongst some of our political African leaders -- or that's the way it seems to your observer, Charles Hayes, this week"................

Nairobi 1960. Kenya's Progress. For BBC:

"I'M STANDING in the heart of the Kenya capital, beside a broad, tarmacadamed highway where, seventy years ago, thousands upon thousands of plains game used to graze. In those days, the animals were undisturbed except perhaps, by a predator, like a lion, or when the silence was broken by a long, sweating, chanting line of caravan porters, on their way to, or from, Uganda.

In the nineties of last century, this was the only way to transport goods through Kenya -- on the heads of toiling, tired men, who made about 12 miles every day, in the 750 mile Mombasa (Kenya Coast) to Uganda journey.

Every modern implement, which went with civilization, travelled over this spot on someone's head. A steel boat, destined to be launched on Lake Victoria, Nyanza, was made in Britain and was left, unassembled, in small pieces, each weighing no more than 60 lbs -- for that was the maximum head load a porter could handle. And the British Chartered company men, who administered Uganda and Kenya in those days, were bankrupted by the huge cost of portage.

At the turn of the century, when the automobile was making its way into British life, one of the Chartered company directors said wistfully, that if the motor vehicle had been invented just 10 years before Britain saw it, we should not have gone broke. It would have reduced our costs by three quarters.

Today, the railway and motor vehicle have welded together East African tribes who were formerly at war with one another. They have driven people into contact, enabling them to travel to areas formerly barred by suspicion and internecine battles.

Passing me in the evening sunshine are streams of African civil servants, going home from their ministry buildings. There are taxis, African-driven, taking tourists just five miles out of the city and enabling the passengers to sit in comfort amongst the lions who still inhabit the plains. There are long-distance coaches, travelling in a few hours the distances that took men three months to accomplish at the turn of the century.

Oil company neon signs, flashing on rooftops, speak silently of the amount of money pouring into government coffers through taxes on fuels and through the enormous industry of tourism, which is built on motor vehicles and will become Kenya's greatest revenue earner.

But there are those who hate the coming of the motorcar --
like the old woman in a tribal district outside the hum of the
towns, who had been waiting for hours to meet the administrator
of her area. He came in his car then soon whisked off. The old
woman said, sadly, "A District Commissioner used to be someone
we could talk to, get advice from. These days, a District
Commissioner is a box on wheels which shouts out of its side."

By the end of the year things were hotting up towards Kenya's
General Election. In his last BBC broadcast for 1960, Charles informed
the world that there was but a month to go before Kenyans would be
visiting the polls.

"This is Charles Hayes reporting to Radio Newsreel and 'BBC
Today', December 1960.
WITH THE GENERAL ELECTION in Kenya only a short time
away, there is growing evidence that some of the dangerous and
more primitive practices of the recent past -- certainly during The
Emergency -- are being revived. Thousands of Kikuyu are being
told, and are believing, that soon European land can be theirs for
the taking.
They are also being told that there is no use, for instance, in
planting crops on their present smallholdings, which have been
built up over the past five years in the huge land consolidation
schemes which put paid to the uneconomic farm system of
fragmented patches. The reason given is, with the return of
Kenyatta, all the new land boundaries must be broken down
again.
They are hearing other things too -- things which are much
more sinister and retrogressive than even this disastrous return to
the past would be. During the years of the Emergency, many girls
have avoided the savage, age-old custom of female circumcision,

which doctors and missionaries have condemned. The reasons were very simple. Many of the 'surgeons' used in these traditional ceremonies had been swept up in the great mass arrests that took place. And, with the business of sheer survival to think about during the Emergency years, these customs -- which were the very basis of tribal structure-- have been forgotten, yet there are stories of women being forced, by public opinion, to submit to the crude and dangerous operation.

This week came the news of a woman who had already borne four children, undergoing the ceremony -- a previously unheard of thing.

Many Kikuyu say that much of the real control in the Kikuyu country now rests in the hands of former Mau Mau men and they say that there is an overall insistence on reversion of the old things. The feeling is so strong that speakers on political platforms praise the idea of a return to the past in an effort to catch votes for the election next month –January 1961.   Reports of the meetings -- held in the Kikuyu language -- is little understood outside the tribe and are sometimes inaccurate. But there is a general feeling that even those Kikuyu who have studied abroad and gained position which education brings, have been forced to pander to this throw-back to the older world of superstition and crippling custom.

Said one prominent Kikuyu in a letter to a newspaper: "Although I am a KANU member, I appeal to all intelligent people in the district to join me to show the KANU leaders that we are not prepared to have another Emergency or a Congo in Kenya."

In all this, of course, there is a Rip Van Winkle attitude -- however appealing it may be to the traditionalists, in being recognized as the next hurdle the Africans have to face.

This is Charles Hayes, in Nairobi, returning you to Radio News Reel."

In October 1960 Charles was sorry to hear (although it was not unexpected), of the demise of England's *News Chronicle*, one of Fleet Street's popular newspapers, when a letter from the *Chronicle*'s foreign news editor, Norman Clark, arrived to inform him of its 'passing'.

Dated 28th October 1960, it read:

"Dear Hayes, You, who were yourself part of the *News Chronicle*, will understand when I say I do not wish to labour words over the paper's passing, bitter and defeated though one feels. Now the paper is no more. To be in Fleet Street is to realize what one felt, but did not appreciate enough before, that the techniques, standards and principles we stood for were the real heart of all good journalism. This is abundantly appreciated now, not only among members of our craft, but also by readers whose letters of despair at the loss of the *News Chronicle* are still coming in, often accompanied by touching postal orders for the staff to have a farewell drink. ...

The Daily Mail has done us the compliment of asking most of our foreign staffers abroad to join them. What I do want to underline is that among our colleagues in the Street, the *News Chronicle* Foreign Service was jealously envied -- Foreign Editors on other papers are now quite frank and open about this when before one only heard it at second hand. And I can now say is what they particularly coveted was our chain of foreign stringers -- second to none as a journalistic team. I have passed your name on, for this reason, to both the "*Mail*" and "*Herald*" Foreign Editors with a strong recommendation that they should consider availing themselves of your services. But I make this proviso: that if I should again find myself in a position where I can build a worldwide chain of stringers, I will call upon you once more........... It remains only for me to thank you for your very loyal and devoted service to the *News Chronicle* and your valued support of myself.

Yours very sincerely, Norman Clark."

On November 2nd, 1961, the British Broadcasting Corporation, (Television Centre), acknowledged and thanked Charles for his help in the pre-filming of Jomo Kenyatta with whom he had contacted and negotiated for the television interview, '*Face to Face*'.

All through the 60's, Charles was sending regular reports to England's *Daily Mail*, *Sketch* and *Sunday Express* newspapers, as well as to popular South African papers.

In February, 1962, Charles went to London to attend the Lancaster House Conference on Kenya's Constitution.

Staying at Ruben's Hotel, on Buckingham Palace Road, he sent out his special Conference Round-up column each evening, which appeared in the *Daily Nation* first edition and in *Taifa Leo* every night. Agence France Presse had taken steps to see that all delegates to the Conference received copies of the *Daily Nation* and *Taifa Leo*, flown into London each day.

From the editor of Mombasa's *East African* newspaper came the message:

"Charles, let me say how very pleased I was to learn that you would be covering the Conference. I can think of no one more suited for the job and with greater understanding of the African scene than you."

Ten-days in England gave Charles the opportunity to meet his daughter Christine, who was a receptionist at London's Cumberland Hotel.

"She had grown up to be a beautiful 20-year-old and it was a pleasure to talk to her and get to know her again. We were determined, this time, to keep in touch."

Later in 1962, with his wife Jean, Charles bought a beachfront lot named 'Giddings' at Shela, on the Arabic island of Lamu, on the Kenya Coast.

Built on the beach, warmed and buffeted by winds from the Indian Ocean, was a roofless, copra barn made of coral that had once belonged to a kindly old man with tufts of white hair growing out of his ears.

He had arrived in the Protectorate in 1912 and was known locally as 'Coconut Charley Whitten', the man who had made a business tearing 'coir'-- the thick, brown fibrous covering -- off the shells of coconuts before selling them. The fibre was then sent to factories to be made into what was known worldwide as hard-wearing 'coconut matting' and rope.

The 'barn' was situated only a few yards back from the highest seawater mark and behind the barn was the almost unbelievable bonus of an ancient fresh water well, right on the beach.

It was Charles' plan to rebuild a house out of the coral barn on the coveted piece of land. But many things to keep them busy were happening at that time, so the planning of a house was put on hold.

The old copra barn at Lamu.

Charles was so fascinated with the history of the island Lamu and Shela that he wrote a piece about the ancient town...Excerpts went like this:

"IN LAMU, you laze with living history -- not in the clinical tabulation of a museum, but with the excitement of being part of an old tableau. It's a different world; a vigorous community going about the work of living in old-world harmony and it begins as soon as dawn leaps into the sky as softly as ballet lighting.

In Lamu the day starts early. What seems to have been quiet streets are suddenly alive with gentle figures -- talkative stevedores quiet for morning prayer; water-taxi men offering safe destinations for passengers; calls of "Makowe, makowe, makowe" and "Siyu, siyu, siyu", uttered softly like the cries of morning birds; cargoes are loaded onto boats -- doum-palm mats, palm oil, copra, ropes, cotton and coconut oil.

Women in dark black robes, ('the all-enveloping 'bui-bui garment, meaning 'spider'), shop diligently in the morning markets, moist, kohl-rimmed eyes probing for bargains; water goes gurgling into lush, walled gardens of tambu, the leaf which adds luxury for betel nut addicts. Sail-makers and ship builders -- keepers of the traditions of centuries -- turn to the work they put down as last evening's muezzin (prayers) called them.

Farmers drive prancing, pattering donkeys from the green open country into the narrow arteries of the town, small panniers of grain and fruit adding pennies to a lax economy. White-walled buildings worship in the sunlight and keep secrets of nights they have known throughout a history colourful with courage and cajoling. Island Lamu is 20 square miles of heaven and even officialdom has been captivated.

Britain and Kenya inherited a turbulent charge, a small island republic, which had seen much violence through the changing ages of East Africa; and whilst they privately despaired of the intrigue and sloth, which characterized life in an Arab state, they fought to keep Lamu the way its people wanted it to remain. Even the prosaic "Outward and Inward Register" of the Sub-Commissioner's office in 1898 tells the story of their work in notes and letters, the Victorian diplomatic niceties of which conceal the violence of days when Lamu controlled the archipelago. As for instance, when the Lamu Commissioner suggested that, to ward off an impending attack on Kiunga by raiding Somalia, the District Officer at Port Durnford should "patrol with soldiers"

In the Jubaland men were being tortured to death -- pegged out with fires lit between their legs. A letter records a non-aggressive complaint from villagers that a "Bwana Masuo" had herded women in chains across the bush from Simambaya to Kiunga.

Yet there is subdued satisfaction in the modest report that a 9 and a half mile road has been built, across warring country in 1898; there is complete administration at work in the "suggestions for a better water supply", sent to Mombasa's Protectorate headquarters; and there is quiet humour in the letter forwarding "charges to be made against officers in hospital", when there was no hospital within 200 miles.

That is the tale of the British connection with Lamu, told today in its results -- the piped water-supply of the town; the spick-and-span hospital on the hill-top; the educational trust set up under the will of Coconut Charlie Witten 'who loved the Lamu children so much'... The Island cried the day this old trader's boat, circling the landing stage for the last time, took him to Mombasa to die in 1953.

But it is not of this comparatively modern history that the sea winds sing in Lamu. They tell of the full-sailed ships which brought colonists from Oman and the Yemen, spilling over into new quieter climes after bickerings and quarrels which split the northern sultanates. They speak of the Banu Il Amu people who gave their name to the island.

In the breeze you may hear of Mrio, the island's first town, buried now under the shifting sands of Hedabu Hill; of early settlers, the Kinamti, who claimed to have been shipwrecked with their cargoes of the first coconut palm seedlings introduced into Lamu; of the heroism of tiny democracies as they warred, five centuries ago, for the Yemeni accoutrements of state -- brass and ivory horns which hang today in the District Commissioner's house. In names in some of the farmsteads amongst the flowering hills back of Lamu Town where you can discover reminders of the Portuguese invaders who made long friendships and conducted punitive expeditions with equal audacity. And sometimes -- especially in neighbouring Siyu, on Patta Island -- you find traces of the marriages between these sea rovers and local beauties, lingering on in Latin olive skins and family names like Orodumila, Waungwama wa Gamia ("the nobles of the camel") and Bombweli.

Older days are remembered by dance teams, which compete on the holidays accompanying harvest sales. Then, colourful costumes and chain-mailed warriors take over the town, to re-live old rivalries, through the narrow streets and along the waterfront from which the life of Lamu derives.

People who go to Lamu fall deeply in love and some -- like old frontier hands Ba Allen, (White Hunter Bunny Allen's older brother), and 'Gerry' Pink, who runs Petley's Inn-- stay to live out their lives there.

The slow evening pace of the lamp lighter, who tends the kerosene lamps of the sea esplanade, is the speed of life, and it suits the lucky ones who can make the break from the towns.

Descendents of the island nobles can afford few of the luxuries of their forebears; but in the little world of Lamu, there is an inbuilt gentility and unexpected courtesies, which mean a welcome for those who seek a heaven on earth."

Charles Hayes. November 1962.

One evening Alan Bobbe, well known in Nairobi for his regular VOK (Voice of Kenya) musical programs and colonial broadcasts, met his friend Charles Hayes at the radio station where Charles was also a frequent broadcaster.

Admitting to Charles that although he enjoyed running his musical programs, what he really wanted to do was to open a small restaurant.

In his youth, Alan Bobbe had learnt standards of culinary excellence at the prestigious Savoy Hotel in London before going on to the Excelsior, in Rome, and then to many other fine hotels and restaurants since.

"If I had the final amount of money now I could buy the perfect place tomorrow," adding, with a smile and a raised eyebrow, "Want to buy my camera, Charles?"

Charles did buy the camera and, in February 1962, Alan opened his restaurant in the heart of Nairobi. 'Bobbe's Bistro', with a service that is still, 40, or so, years later, highly personalized, having set the standards by which many Kenya restaurants are judged.

Some of his clientele include Bing Crosby, Peter Ustinov, Sydney Poitier, Walter Cronkite, as well as famous food writers, Dukes and their Duchesses and the crème de la crème of East African tourists.

NINETEEN

Realising a Dream

"The Isle is full of noises, sounds and sweet airs,
that give delight and hurt not."
W. Shakespeare, *The Tempest*

BY 1963 CRESCENT ISLAND, the high curved rim of an ancient crater, set in Lake Naivasha in Kenya's Great Rift Valley, was for sale and it was this island that Jean Hayes had first seen, and fallen in love with, after landing by flying boat in Lake Naivasha back in the '50's.

As a 'weekend' ornithologist, it was her dream to one day live on that 600-acre island of grassy slopes, dotted with umbrella-like acacia trees, (mimosa), whose yellow blossoms smelt so sweetly at certain times of the year.

She longed to watch and photograph the birds and to study the wild life, like hippopotamuses, who heaved themselves from the lake waters before trundling heavily onto the island, at night, to graze.

She wanted to look with wonder at nearby giraffe, gazelles, zebra and chubby waterbuck wandering at will beneath shady trees, where occasionally, at dusk, a leopard stalked.

Charles, as Kenyan citizen number 4019, was legally entitled to own land, so Crescent Island was purchased, by his company, from a man called Ernie Hammer, with the object of Charles and Jean Hayes to declare it a wildlife and bird sanctuary.

World famous ornithologists, Dr. Roger Tory Peterson and John Williams, while on safari in Kenya at separate times, found that over 400 varieties of fresh water birds nested regularly on Crescent Island.

(There are over 1400 in Kenya).   So Charles, with the help of John Williams, edited the small brochure *The Birds of East Africa,* written especially for visiting ornithologists and interested local bird watchers.

A large house had already been built on the crest of the island that Charles and Jean moved into, mainly for occasional bird and animal watching, while still maintaining their Riverside Drive house in Nairobi, 50 miles away.

Jean was still managing Andrew Crawford Productions Ltd. in Nairobi, which had been relocated from Jevanjee Street, in the city's overcrowded centre, to the quieter area of Government Road, a short way out of town, while Charles enjoyed his editorial directorship of the *Nation Series* newspapers in Victoria Street, (later changed to Tom Mboya Street).

That month, a letter published in one of Nairobi's Sunday newspapers came from His Highness the Aga Khan, Paris, which read:

"Sir, My attention has been drawn to the report, "Aga Khan supports Kenyatta," last Sunday. I am afraid it conveys an entirely wrong impression in relation to my position as religious head of the Ismaili Muslims.

Whilst I am a shareholder in the Company which owns the *Daily Nation*, all matters of policy are decided locally in Nairobi and are no concern of the shareholders and are matters for the Editor. When it came to my knowledge that the Editor proposed to support Mr. Kenyatta, I made it clear that in my position I am not concerned at all with party politics, but I believe that an Editor is entitled to support any political party which he thinks will act in the best interests of his country. I should be obliged if you would make it clear, as religious head of the Ismaili Muslims, I cannot become involved in party politics. Aga Khan. June. 1963."

This letter appeared in the same publication:

"Sir, The Aga Khan does not issue editorial instructions; but my main concern is to refute your correspondent's colourful suggestion that, following an alleged "approach" by Mr Kenyatta, some devious plot was hatched in Bombay eight months ago which would ensure K.A.N U. (Kenya National African Union), the support of the *Daily Nation* or the Ismaili community. This is utter nonsense."
Michael H. Curtis. Managing Director, East African Newspapers, Nairobi, Kenya.

On June 1st 1963, Kenya attained internal self-government. Named Madaraka Day -- meaning 'promotion' in the Kiswahili language, Jomo Kenyatta was sworn in as Kenya's Prime Minister.

Just three days before, on May 28th, Jomo Kenyatta, then the KANU president, had been called on by the Governor General of Kenya, Malcolm MacDonald, to form the new government as Kenya's first Prime Minister.

By the end of that year, 12th December 1963, when Kenya became fully independent, a personal message, with a coloured photograph of the Prime minister, was sent out on post cards all over the country from the Hon. J. Kenyatta M.N.A., Prime Minister of Kenya. It read:

"I send the good wishes of the people of Kenya to the people of all countries of the world on the joyous occasion of our long-awaited Independence, on 12th December 1963."

To mark the historic event of Kenya's attainment of self-government a complete new issue of 14 postage stamps was placed on sale.

That same week, on December 10th 1963, the Island of Zanzibar became an Independent nation.

By the 16th of that month Zanzibar joined the United Nations, but less than a month later the Zanzibar government was overthrown by a young Ugandan named John Okello, who had dreams of grandeur of becoming the great nationalist who overthrew the Sultan of Zanzibar.

Okello, with the men who had rallied round him all armed with weapons, soon defeated the Sultan's troops and self-styled Field Marshal John Okello broadcast his message to the people of Zanzibar;

"I am Field Marshal John Okello! Wake up you imperialists. There is no longer an imperialist government on this island. Wake up, you black men. Let everyone of you take a gun and start to fight."

Later that day Okello issued an ultimatum to the Sultan, which read:

"You are allowed 20 minutes to kill your children and wives then to kill yourself."

But the Sultan and his family had escaped secretly to neighbouring Tanzania where urgent arrangements had been made for them, by England, for their safety.

As the news broke, Charles, always in search of top news, hired a plane and pilot, taking off immediately from Nairobi to Zanzibar Island.

As the small plane circled the airport, Charles could see that huge oil barrels had been rolled across the runway. Talking to the control officer, a white man who the pilot could see quite clearly as they were flying so low, they were advised to get away as soon as possible.

Suddenly all contact stopped and the pilot and Charles actually saw the man in the control tower being dragged away by Africans.

"There was nothing we could do. There was no place to land safely."

The revolution was over in 24 hours, but by the third day it was estimated that hundreds of people who had fought against the revolution had been killed and there were many more civilians who could not be found. Although the fighting didn't last long, the Zanzibar Revolution was, up to that time, the most violent in tropical African history.

Charles had much to report on the BBC news that night.

A few days later, (December 1963), the following BBC report from Charles in Nairobi pinpointed Somalia:

"THE REPUBLIC OF SOMALIA is a hard, scorching, cruel tract of sand and rock from which the citizens scratch food and life in a tough, never-ending fight for survival. They have a pattern of migrations between the water-holes and the grazing grounds, which has gone on for centuries, and they ignore the neat lines on maps drawn by the 19th Century civilization, which intruded into their way of life. But to develop Somalia into a food-producing area would require immense resources -- greater probably than in any other part of Africa. Oil would be the great saviour and exploration companies have poured money into the Republic in the search for the black gold. None has been found in economic quantities.

The only other answer seems obvious therefore to the Somalia people -- the attachment of lands, which were included, by various boundary commissions, in neighbouring countries like Ethiopia and Kenya.

The project to change the national map for the Horn of Africa is called the "Greater Somalia Plan" and lush grazing grounds in the southeastern part of Ethiopia are the major targets.

Northern Kenya -- dry, sandy and vast -- represents a sort of national home, in which 60,000 more Somalis live.

French Somaliland, with the port of Djibouti, is the 5th segment of the Plan to be achieved. So, since it required full independence from Italian and British colonizers three years ago, Somalia has been shopping around for assistance. Not only economic aid was requested, but Somalia wanted guns and it wanted to expand its standing army of 5,000 men.

Countries like the United States, Western Germany and Italy -- willing to help -- advised that the economic conditions of the country could not support a larger army.

'Let's first improve your food-growing capacity, your health and educational facilities, your communications and your ports,' they said.

West Germany settled down to build roads; the United States put in a 5-million dollar improvement program for the little harbour of Kismayu; the six countries of the European Economic Community built a six-storey hospital just outside the Somali capital, Moygadishu. Egypt helped with education.

Then came the diplomatic collapse of relations between Britain and Somalia -- because Britain refused to amputate Kenya territory and give it to Somalia.

With this action came the drying up of one and one half million English pounds, which Britain gave annually to Somalia in order to balance its precarious budget.

The Somalia president, Dr. Shermarke, made a quick trip to Peking and almost bridged the gap in aid from Communist China. Moreover, a defense agreement was concluded with China and long-term interest-free loans agreed. Russia promised a 14 million

Pound agricultural programme. But still this was not enough. Somalia sought massive military aid -- and last week, she got it – 11 million Pounds worth from Russia, which was apparently anxious to outdo anything China could achieve.

When Somalia thereafter rejected offers made by western countries, the Communist dream of a pincer movement both in East and West Africa became more of a concrete fact.

The result is that Somalia can look aggressively west, at Ethiopia, and south, towards Kenya, from which the British military base will be withdrawn when full independence comes in December. The army of the Somalia Republic will leap from 5,000 men to 20,000 with Russian militarists to train them.

In Ethiopia, there is already alarm. The Emperor, Haile Selassie, has pointed out that military expansion of this sort is beyond any reasonable requirement for internal security and the consequence of the creation of an army of this size may be to provide basic conditions for another Korea.

'Patience,' warned the Emperor, 'is not without limits.'

In Kenya the message of communist strategy is getting home to them quietly -- no longer a theory against which western propaganda has been directed, but a real threat. As an observer put it this week:

'The tragedy is that, when the showdown eventually comes, it will be Africans killing Africans, as they are doing in the Sahara. Border raids are already increasing.'

Yet if the military build-up leads to aggression, then Kenya will not stand alone. The proposed East African army command will probably involve Tanganyika and Uganda. Ethiopia will probably also take immediate defensive action -- unless the strength of the movement for African unity can prevail over aggressive intent.

So far, there has been no demonstration of the success of any such policy and Africa has no unified force with which to enforce its policy of peace.

In Kenya, the projection of the East-West struggle, into Africa in military terms, is seen as the factor most calculated to alarm the African continent into the most positive action it has yet taken and big decisions are expected from the headquarters of the movement for African unity when heads of state meet there soon.

The springboard of military power, which Somalia now represents, will cause repercussions everywhere. This is Charles Hayes in Nairobi, returning you to London."

In the New Year, Charles received a letter from his daughter, Christine, asking if he would come to London to 'give her away' at her marriage to Alwyn Spencer Douglas Rougier-Chapman, on March 14th, 1964.

"I was being pulled in all directions at that time," said Charles, "and, although my heart was with Christine, I was unable to get to her wedding, which took place at St James Church, Spanish Place, London. But we were in touch, and that was important to me."

The newlyweds spent their honeymoon in Spain, afterwards moving to Brussels where they lived for six years. Charles' first two grandsons, Andrew and Duncan, were born there.

The Rougier-Chapman family moved to Grand Rapids, Michigan, USA, in 1970.

Alwyn Rougier-Chapman marries Charles' first daughter, Christine, on March 14th, 1964, at St. James Church, Spanish Place, London.

TWENTY

A New President

"You may be judged by History for your political actions,
but you will be judged by God for the spirit which is in your heart."
Oliver Baldwin

ON OCTOBER 18th, 1964, named Jamhuri Day, Jomo Kenyatta became the Republic of Kenya's new President, surprising many observers by leading Kenya into a period of economic growth and unexpected tribal harmony. A remarkable mixture of Kikuyu Nationalist, pragmatic politician and father figure, President Jomo Kenyatta was known fondly throughout the country as, Mzee, (a respected and wise old man).

At the lavish Kenya Uhuru celebrations, held in Nairobi, when tribal dancing, huge coloured lights and fireworks were watched by thousands of thrilled and excited Kenyans and visiting dignitaries from all over the world, there was, at midnight, a long moment of silence when the British flag was gradually lowered to give place to the Kenya flag.

Beneath the stars, the flag fluttered gently in a warm evening breeze, showing proudly its black, red and green; Kenyan crowds and visitors roared their happiness. Representing Britain, Prince Phillip, Duke of Edinburgh, stood beside President Jomo Kenyatta. At this historic moment Prince Phillip, well known for his dry humour, quipped quietly, "Mr Kenyatta, are you sure you don't want to change your mind!"

The Prince was answered by a quiet chuckle from Kenya's new President.

England's Prince Philip waves to the crowd at Kenya's independence celebrations, (Uhuru). (pic: *Daily Nation*)

That year Charles purchased a farm adjacent to Crescent Island, joining the two pieces of land by building a short causeway over the water. Naming it Sanctuary Farm, giraffe, various buck and zebra were then able to walk freely and safely across to the island from land and forests quickly being occupied by African farmers and cultivated flower growers; a new venture for Naivasha at that time.

Charles then decided to buy, from local rancher Peter Gaymer, 50 steers, for the price of Ksh 20,000.

He made his African farmer friend, Peter Khama, his partner, and from then on Khama managed the whole farming business, adding acres of vegetables and building a milk shed for Jersey cows he had bought with farm profits.

The original farmhouse was a delightful building surrounded by huge, dark-green Euphorbia (candelabrum) trees. (When these dramatic, succulent tree branches are broken, a milky, rubber-like substance drips out -- dangerous should it get into the eyes).

There were always human-interest stories to follow so, with news-nose twitching, Charles heard that well-known South African singer, Miriam Makeba, would be arriving shortly in Tanzania to give a special performance.

"I travelled to Tanzania ready to get a news story and pictures, but was very surprised that there was no one at the Dar–a-Salaam airport to greet her. Had I got the date wrong?

"As the plane touched down I stood back, thinking that a welcoming committee would suddenly appear, but there was no one in sight. Miriam Makeba alighted from the plane with her back-up of glamorous African singers and, to an empty airport, except for me and the air crew, they burst into her famous Zulu, (South African), 'click' song.

"Embarrassed for them, I took them in a taxi to the government-owned Dar Hotel where the manager, just as embarrassed as I was, led the now furious singing group to their rooms while I tried to raise someone in the information department. There was no one in the office, so I rang the Vice President's house. Only giggling children answered.

"Returning to the hotel I joined the manager and Miriam Makeba for dinner, managing to get pictures and her story which I quickly buzzed off to the *Daily Nation* under the head line; 'Nyerere Ignores Makeba'.

"Miriam Makeba had travelled half-way round the world, from London, to New York, to East Africa, especially to sing to the Tanzanians whom she admired. She had already asked permission of President Nyerere if she may become a Tanzanian citizen.

"After such a rebuff as a non-event arrival in Tanzania, Miriam Makeba and her entourage left for Tunisia the following morning where, it was heard, she later became a citizen of that country."

Newspaper journalism and magazine production took much of his time, but Charles also edited, for several months, the noted glossy wild animal conservation magazine, '*Africana*'. For this he was presented, in 1964, a set of 24 Franklin Mint gold medallions --each with the imprint of an African wild animal on it. The velvet-lined, boxed set was awarded to Charles from the East African Wild Life Society 'for services to wildlife conservation'.

It was in 1964 that events occurred which would alter the course of Charles' life dramatically.

TWENTY-ONE

A Meeting Meant-To-Be

"When Love and Skill work together, expect a Masterpiece."
John Ruskin

FROM A TAPE RECORDING, made many years later, Charles explained how the year 1964 changed his life:

"One warm Sunday evening, in mid-1964, I drove a few miles out of Nairobi to the small village of Kiambu where there was a coffee farm advertised for sale. I became lost in the maze of coffee bushes that stretched out before me.

Seeing a house at the end of a dividing road I knocked on the open door hoping to find directions. When the lady, who I thought owned the house, looked at me I found that I was stammering like an idiot when simply asking to use the telephone.

I had heard it said, and had poo-pooed it, that love at first sight feels like a bolt of lightening hitting you at full blast, yet here was I, nearing 50 years old and spinning with electricity while standing on the doorstep of a woman I had just met.

As I stood cranking the handle of an old-fashioned Kenya telephone, fixed shoulder-height to the wall, she sat cross-legged on a sofa, tapping away at a typewriter.

She wore a brightly coloured African kikoi wrapped round her. Long hair brushed her shoulders. While waiting for the call to come through, I had time to watch her. She was stunning. Then I had the audacity to ask what she was working on.

She said, easily, with a wide smile, 'My last fashion column for next week's *Sunday Post* before going on leave to England for three months. But I shall be sending an '*On Safari*' column each week until I return.'

Then my call came through. Thanking her, I stumbled into my car. Feeling dazed, I drove away, forgetting all about the coffee farm."

Each week, for the next three months, Charles bought the *Sunday Post* newspaper.

"I had found her name was Margaret Burke and, through her safari columns, knew where she was travelling, but wondering, all the while, what the outcome would be.

"There's always small-talk about life's coincidences, and meant-to-be occasions, but the following September I was to attend a meeting of agriculturalists at the old Bell Inn, Naivasha, to discuss what I intended planting on Crescent Island. The previous owners had grown potatoes there, but I was not interested in crops -- only in making a sanctuary for wild animals and birds."

In his coffee-and-cream convertible Mercedes, Charles drew up to the stone verandah at the inn.

"To my amazement I saw that 'she', Margaret Burke, was sitting there amongst the group of agriculturalists. I almost tripped up the steps. We looked at each other, knowing immediately and without doubt, it was the most over-powering experience that had ever happened to either of us. I don't remember a thing about the meeting.

"But it would be another eight loving years, after the birth of our daughter Caroline Rima in February 1966, before it became the right moment for us to be married -- a third time for us both."

Charles with five-year-old Caroline who says, "I'll twist your ears off if you don't buy me some sweets."

For Charles the following years proved to be full of interest and change.

In September 1965 his broadcast to America from Nairobi, (on *ABC*), welcomed two United States astronauts to Kenya:

"TODAY, Kenya's President, Jomo Kenyatta, welcomed United States' astronauts Gordon Cooper and Charles Conrad to his country. They arrived from Madagascar on a whistle-stop tour of Africa. An album of photographs, they presented to Jomo Kenyatta, showing how the huge slash in the earth's surface, called the Great Rift Valley, looked to them during their momentous eight days of space flight last month.

All through Nairobi, its streets bright with the many-hued bougainvillea which grow in profusion in the City centre, people ran out of offices and shops to cheer as the astronauts' motorcade passed on their way to the House of Assembly, where members of parliament waited to meet them.

Then a flight over the parched earth, where it plunges into the Great Rift Valley, was arranged for the astronauts. The nearest these men had previously been to this great crack in the earth's crust was 100 miles above, but now they could see the bare bosom of the hills as they flew low over the scrubby cover of Maasailand. Below, circles of thorn enclosed a manyatta -- a Maasai village of houses made with mud and cattle dung; dry river beds biting deep into the red earth; cattle trails made during the long, drought-stricken year and plumes of smoke drifting leisurely from bush fires which eat their way through the dry brush.

Cooper and Conrad, accompanied by William Attwood, United States Ambassador in Nairobi, looked down over the rusty-red-coloured earth and at the tiny airstrip of Keekorok, set in lusher grazing lands which the Maasai have reserved for Kenya's huge herds of wild game.

Alongside the airstrip, at Keekorok, a guard of honour was drawn up for the two astronauts -- but guards with a very big difference. These were the Maasai -- men from the tribe which refuses to enter the hurly-burly life of the modern world. They still, in this 20th century, wear red ochre in their hair and over their oiled bodies in preference to clothes. They live the lives of nomads, following their cattle in the search for good grazing in this dry country. And they are prepared to offer their lives in the protection of those cattle -- tackling marauding lion with nothing but spear and painted shield, made from the tough hide of the buffalo which are here in their thousands.

The Maasai stood guard to honour men whose exploits they can only faintly comprehend. Thirty-eight year-old Gordon Cooper -- slim and five foot eight inches high -- is dwarfed by some of these young warriors who stare at him with their slanted eyes as he leads the way. The younger Charles Conrad stands slightly in the rear, smiling as the Maasai leap high in the air.

Through ranks of zebra and frisky wildebeest, tall spotted giraffe and blackberry-blue-rumped topi, they passed to Keekorok Safari Lodge, declared officially open only a few hours before. And there, at the edge of the verandah, stood President Jomo Kenyatta, one of Africa's elder statesmen at ease in his trilby hat and his beach shirt.

The Maasai stopped their dancing, to stare, curious but unperturbed, at the men from outer space. There was disappointment that Cooper and Conrad were not wearing the capsule itself.

Then the President took two burnished Maasai spears, handing them across to the astronauts with the words,

'For your bravery I give you these spears, the spears of victory -- and remember such spears are sharp.'

Then he took the astronauts and their families out to the game area, which surrounds the Lodge, insisting that they should see a lion before they left Kenya.

The Maasai watched, neither comprehending what it was all about nor the point of it all. Their only care is whether there is grass on the moon for cattle.

But for the rest of Kenya, this fleeting visit, by two unassuming young men, was the tops. Charles Hayes, Nairobi, for ABC."

President of Kenya, Jomo Kenyatta, welcomes American astronauts, Charles Conrad and Gordon Cooper, presenting each a glinting Maasai spear. (pic: *Daily Nation*)

Sometime that year, Joy Adamson arrived in Nairobi from a bush camp having decided to leave her husband George there for a while with his lions. Fed up with living inside a huge caged enclosure -- while the lions lived outside the cage-- she wanted a permanent home.

Charles knew there was a house for sale on the shores of Lake Naivasha, so suggested driving Joy there to look at it.

"As we walked down the driveway, a troop of Colobus monkeys, their long tails and black and white furry capes swishing high amongst the branches of acacia trees, screeched, in their harsh, staccato voices, what Joy felt was her welcome. Throwing her arms in the air, eyes wide open, she shouted, 'Thees ees it!'"

Back in Nairobi Joy talked to her accountant Peter Johnson (of Gill and Johnson) who, after looking at the Naivasha house with her, decided that some of the Elsa (Lion) Trust money could buy the property.

Within weeks Joy moved into the Lakeside house, naming it "Elsamere".

By November that year, Charles, as editorial director of the Nation Group of Newspapers, was offered a seat on Pan Am's inaugural flight from Nairobi to New York.

"More than anything New York had to offer, I really enjoyed late-night, sometimes all-night, jazz concerts. It was an experience not to be missed," he said on his return to Nairobi.

Later that year Charles recorded a series of 45rpm disks on tribal drumming and East African bird song. Also he was the narrator of a 35rpm disk named 'Wild Africa' on which some of the most dramatic wild animal sounds had been recorded by Jean Hayes and one of Kenya's small force of appointed honorary game wardens, Jan Otto Allen. For each recorded disk sold, the publishers, Andrew Crawford Productions Ltd., contributed funds to the East African Wild Life Society. The cover, from a painting by well-known artist Joyce Butter, helped to promote the truly recorded sound of lion, rhino, buffalo, elephant, leopard, cheetah, hyena and savage wild dogs. "Wild Africa is your Safari in Sound," it read.

The record (disk) sold well to tourists and Kenyan residents.

In 1966 Charles' old friend, Uganda's first president, the Kabaka, (King), Frederick Mutesa the Second, somehow upset the country's prime minister, Milton Obote.
Mobilised by Obote, a military force surrounded the popular 'King Freddie's' palace, which, for a start, was an insult to the Kabaka's people, the Baganade.
At dead of night, King Freddie escaped through a hole in the royal fence and was not heard of for several weeks as he made his way, incognito, across the border to Kenya. In the coup other members of Buganda's royal family were scattered.
In Nairobi, one early morning, Charles found that the Kabaka's brother, Prince Henry Kimera of Buganda, had pitched up on his doorstep.
"Looking disheveled and bearded I didn't recognise him at first," said Charles. "The Prince was dressed in an old navy sweater with holes in the elbows and a pair of ragged jeans which, he told me later, he had acquired from one of his loyal subjects. He explained how Obote's secret police force had been sent to track him down and obliterate him, so he had come through back roads and forests to stay with me, hopefully in safety, until he could get to England.
"Because he was a political 'hot potato', sensitive, diplomatic niceties were involved by his arrival, so I telephoned high-level government sources and within 30 minutes Kenya's Vice President Daniel Arap Moi walked into my living room, in Riverside Drive."
Well aware that Charles was a British Broadcasting Corporation 'stringer', Arap Moi warned,

"If a word of this leaks out, Charles, you're in trouble, but it would be advisable that Prince Henry should stay with you until we can arrange his next move."

After dark, every night for the next two weeks, Charles took the royal guest out on a search of bus depots and Nairobi's railway station for the distressed man's wife, the Princess, and their children, who were also trying to make their way to safety.

Large numbers of Ugandans and Kenyans were also fleeing Uganda, bringing horrifying stories of carnage taking place in the capital city of Kampala and its environs.

"At last, one evening, Prince Henry found his family dressed as beggars, alighting from a country bus. They all moved into my house to await instructions from our VP Arap Moi," said Charles.

Every day Charles filed protected pieces to BBC, giving eyewitness accounts of widespread murder, the dumping of dead bodies in mass graves and into Lake Victoria (Nyanza province). "Ugandan crocodiles are being well fed, and travellers are terrified," he reported.

As a result of Charles' protected reports, a BBC television crew flew out to Nairobi but were turned back at the Ugandan border, so Kenyan government permitted a film interview with the united royal family, provided it was not telecast until President Kenyatta lifted the news blackout.

A letter to Prince Henry from England's Home Office in Whitehall on 29th June 1966, read:

"Dear Prince Henry, You wrote to the Home Secretary on the 24th June to ask that your wife might be given an entry certificate to enable her to come to the United Kingdom. I am writing to say that the Home Secretary has authorized the issue of an entry certificate and that the British High Commission in

Nairobi is being asked to get in touch with your wife for the purpose. Yours sincerely, D.E.J.Dowler. Whitehall. London."

By now the Kabaka, King Frederick, had reached London and attempts were made to help his brother Prince Henry and his family to join him there. "But there were irritating delays in the immigration process," said Charles, "so by the time arrangements had been completed, and I had seen the Ugandan family safely on their way out of Kenya, other news media had picked up the royal travellers at London's Heathrow airport, beating BBC to what should have been an exclusive."

Uganda's royal family settled down safely in Britain, but Prince Henry must have been devastated to watch his brother, King Freddie, drink himself towards poverty, and eventual death, a few years later.

President of Tanzania, Julius Nyerere, President of Kenya, Jomo Kenyatta and President of Uganda, Milton Obote, in London. (pic: *Daily Nation*)

Vice President of Kenya, Daniel Arap Moi, is introduced by Charles to the film cast of 'Cowboy in Africa' at the film's premiere at the Globe Theatre, Nairobi, 1967. (pic: *Daily Nation*)

Charles Hayes, with Margaret, hosts a television quiz program for *Schweppes* in Nairobi. 1965. (pic: *Daily Nation*)

During Pan Am's inaugural flight to New York from Nairobi, Mamma Ngina Kenyatta, wife of the President of Kenya, meets Mrs. Lyndon B. Johnson, wife of the U.S. President, in Washington. 1966 (pic: CH)

The Nation, Charles' newspaper, advertised on a country roadside at Msambweni, on the Kenya Coast. 1999.

TWENTY-TWO

Lifestyle Change

"In politics, if you want anything said, ask a man.
If you want anything done, ask a woman."
Margaret Thatcher

IN 1969, TIRING OF THE STRESS AND STRAIN of life in a city that was frustrating him beyond measure, Charles thought deeply about living in Naivasha, where he owned property.

He decided to transfer ownership of Crescent Island to a small consortium set up under the name Lake Naivasha Enterprises Limited, (LNE).

Michael Dunford, who owned a large cliff top house on land adjoining Sanctuary Farm, and Nairobi businessman, Jimmy Virjee, were the other shareholders. Companies within the group included the Bell Inn Limited, Naivasha Marina Club, Oserian Development Company Limited and The Mombasa Marina Limited, headed by chairman Michael Dunford.

With tourism in Kenya looking up, shareholders could see the possibilities of running an upcountry, Lakeside Marina Club with Charles as manager. Furthermore, a film company was making interested noises about shooting a film in the Naivasha area, so Charles and the directors of California's 'Open Road Films' talked about Crescent Island and its forested surrounds as a possible location.

"If you would build some houses to accommodate our stars and film crew, and allow us to erect tents and cages on Sanctuary farm for our animals and their handlers, we would seriously consider shooting the film '*Living Free*' here," said the film company directors.

As Charles had already resigned his editorial directorship of the Nation Group of Newspapers, he was now excited about the idea of opening and managing a Marina Club which would enable him to spend more time in the fresh air of Naivasha. But he hadn't, up to then, envisaged a Californian film company being even remotely interested in making a film around the lake. That, he mused, would be a bonus indeed.

By the time Lake Naivasha Marina Club opened, on December 1st, 1969, with a membership of 90 couples, sufficient mooring berths for their boats and thatched weekend houses, (bandas), had already been built for them in stone by a talented crew of African artisans who Charles had gathered together.

Another interesting venture had beckoned LNE shareholders. A large white 'palace' of Spanish design, built in 1927 by Cyril Ramsey-Hill on the shore of Lake Naivasha, just a few miles away from the Marina Club, was for sale. Its domes and castellations were beginning to fall apart as it became more derelict. The building, known as '*Oserian*', a Maasai name meaning 'Place of Peace' belonged to Diana, Lady Delamere; her husband, Lord Delamere, being Kenya's largest landowner. The couple farmed further along the lake.[15]

After a meeting of LNE shareholders, the Company bought 'Oserian' (locally named The Gin Palace, later renamed Djinn Palace), for the asking price of 30,000 UK pounds. With the building went 5,000 acres of 'wild Africa' where buffalo, zebra, giraffe, plains game and an assortment of smaller animals roamed. Charles suggested that the whole place could be set up as a type of Club Mediterranean, with luxury all the way.

---

[15] A film, "White Mischief", partly shot at 'Oserian', in Naivasha in the 80's, showed how the murder of Lady Delamere's lover, the Earl of Errol, took place in 1947. The film was released a few years after her death.

Plans for its future were in slow progress but, with excitement mounting, rumours round the lake took off at an amazing pace. "Oh," said one source, "it is going to be a Play Boy club!" On hearing this, Charles muttered into his Scotch that evening, "they wish."

Oserian, the Djinn Palace, on the shore of Lake Naivasha, circa 1960.

With little time for Charles to 'take a deep breath', plans for 'Oserian' were put aside after receiving a letter from California which stated that the film company had definitely decided to organize their move to Kenya by late 1970.

Charles had to move quickly, getting his African builders and plumbers into position again to complete the order for extra housing. Plans made for extending the house at Sanctuary Farm, which was to be turned into offices for the film company, had to be processed and, on the farm land itself, areas under large acacia 'umbrella' shade trees were to be made ready for erecting cages for the lions, and other wild animal stars, with a luxury tented camp set out nearby for their handlers and trainers.

A restaurant, large enough to seat at least a hundred people, was designed by Charles whose large labour force hacked oblong chunks of yellow stone from Sanctuary Farm quarry with which to build it.

"There was no time to lose," said an excited Charles.

Plans went ahead to build the restaurant on top of the cliff overlooking the Lake, offering a 'million dollar view', in anyone's opinion, he decided. And he was right.

The restaurant, built in two levels, curved grandly into a crescent shape to complement the island, which could be seen from the open-sided building.

By the time furnishings and kitchen equipment had been purchased and put into place, 24 newly-trained African waiters were ready, although a trifle nervous, to make sure that club members and the American film makers and their 'stars', were well looked after. Each waiter wore black trousers, white shirts and burgundy felt waistcoats embroidered in yellow down the front, and was crowned with a burgundy fez, (flowerpot-shaped hat), with a yellow tassel hanging on one side.

A well-stocked bar was made from a large wooden boat set five feet down into a cool concrete floor in the lounge so that drinks could be served at bar seat level -- the barman standing in the boat below.

Within a year the film company arrived, so it was with relief that the weather remained hot and dry -- as it usually is at Christmas time in Kenya -- because the restaurant roof had not been completed!

An African thatching crew was rushed in for an overtime job and, with much laughter, and rhythmic singing, they went about cutting marula, (papyrus), from the lake edge, putting it into great bathtubs of water to soften it, then, with a clever twist of each papyrus stem, the men were up ladders holding armfuls of the roofing material, entwining it firmly through the wooden lathes, already fixed with precision, in lines across the skeleton of the restaurant roof.

The men worked all through the warm starry night, stopping only for great bowls of hot curried goat, vegetables and rice carried from the kitchens by a fleet of new African cooks headed by the best mpishi (cook), of all; the plump-faced, smiling Absolem, from the Abaluya tribe. Besides all his other culinary attributes, he was a master at making milk-bread rolls.

By morning the roof was a work of art. Visitors popped into the Club especially to see for themselves the unique way papyrus thatching was done.

But Charles' next building venture -- an egg-shaped swim pool -- was not the best thing to have happened. Although it turned out to be the largest pool in Naivasha, whatever chemicals were used and work done to make it attractive to swimmers, it never became clean and blue like normal pools. Charles threw up his hands in despair when members' children put live lake fish and water snakes into the pool's murky depths, creating havoc and panic especially when female club members entered the pool -- at their own risk, it was advised. The pool never did work properly, so eventually was filled in and, in desperation, covered with fast-growing lawn seed.

Everything had been completed by the time the main film actors arrived; Susan Hampshire, who was to take the part of Joy Adamson, and Nigel Davenport who was to play that of her husband, George Adamson.

The film company stayed about a year to complete their film, '*Living Free*', during which time the large lion, 'Thunder', one of the main stars of the film, lived in a room-sized cage on Crescent Island. Every night and early morning his roars echoed around the lake, thrilling everyone who heard him. Director of the film, Jack Couffer, rented Crescent Island house.

Charles and his wife Jean took part in the film as tourists on safari, terrified of hearing what they imagined was a lion -- at least a man-eater, outside their tent. In the film Charles is seen taking his gun, bravely, to frighten the animal away but, by mistake, shoots a milk bottle off the table! The scary lion turned out to be a very small lion, with big round eyes, eventually peeping shyly round the tent flap, bringing laughter from audiences.

Just weeks later there came a moment of supreme happiness for Charles when he received a telegram from his son, Michael, asking if they could spend some time together, especially as it was nearing his 21st birthday.

"Delighted beyond measure," said Charles, "I went to meet him at Nairobi airport, wondering if I would recognize him after so many of his growing-up years or, if indeed, he would recognize me. He was only 14 years old when last we had met, during one of my rare visits to London."

There was no need for undue worry. Friends of Charles, also waiting for British Airways passengers to alight, exclaimed, pointing, "Charles, that young man must be your son. He looks exactly like you!"

The days and weeks following were mind-boggling as father and son found much in common.

A decision was soon made that Michael would stay at the Marina for a while to help with the film company. And Michael certainly proved his worth as he drove old lorries, (vehicles Charles had bought cheaply at questionable auctions), that were breaking down constantly, and long wheel-based Land Rovers filled with huge tents for film stars and crew members to sit beneath, shaded and in comfort, for their mid-day meals and coffee breaks out in the bush where every few days a different location was used.

Tents that had to be erected and dismantled daily were only few of the problems confronting Michael and his African helpers. There were chairs and folding tables to be packed for well over fifty people comprising of film and sound crew, actors, make-up artists, hairdressers and drivers. Added to that, two gas stoves and their cylinders, (for heating daily 'hot' lunches demanded by the film company who also wanted the choice of a cold buffet lunch), plates, cups, knives, forks, spoons and table napkins and, of course, the actual three–course meals already cooked early morning, by Absolum in the Marina Club kitchens.

All equipment and especially the food carried on the vehicles had to be battened down with strong covers and rope to keep thick, choking red dust from infiltrating everything as it was bumped and rattled, most times over unmade-up roads and tracks, often shuddering into ant-bear holes.

For some of the film crew, who had never before left England or the States, where their city lives ran smoothly on tarmac roads, each day became a constant fear of maybe meeting snakes or spiders, being eaten by 'something' or getting malaria from the dreaded mosquitoes; an enigma which took weeks for them to unravel. But cool evenings back at the Club, after soothing drinks and dinner, often developed into many hilarious hours that stretched into late night as film makers and crew huddled round the bar discussing the amazing happenings of a day spent under an African sun, while Charles and Michael, and Margaret's youngest son, Roger Sylvester, being the charming hosts they were, smoothed away any possible upsets that might have occurred.

"All told, the whole year was pretty stressful," said Charles.

"I was not familiar with running a Marina Club full of people, many of them film actors and film makers. Although it was great fun some of the time, and we made a few lifelong friends, it was with relief when the film company packed up to return to the States."

Lake Naivasha Club cliff top. Crescent Island can be seen in background.

Young Caroline oversees new buildings at the Marina Club.

Aerial view of Crescent Island.

JAMBO, SAYS MR TOWETT

Mr. Taita Towett outgrowls young film star Safi when the two met at the Marina Club at Lake Naivasha on Saturday. Mr. Towett, the Minister for Education was introduced to Safi who is here from America to play a leading role in the film "Living Free" which will star Susan Hampshire as Joy Adamson and Nigel Davenport as George. The film is based on Joy Adamson's best-selling sequel to "Born Free" which was also filmed in Kenya. Filming begins later this year and the young lions are currently being acclimatised. (Photo: MB Ltd.)

Nigel Davenport and Susan Hampshire on the set of 'Living Free', Naivasha. Below: One of the lion stars on set at Sanctuary Farm. (pic: CH)

Lion star of the film 'Living Free' relaxes with Charles on the Marina Club steps. (Pic: M.B.Ltd.)

In November 1972, Charles was cast as a white hunter named 'Jock McEwan' in yet another film, with the working title, "The Biggest Bongo in Africa" (later named '*In Search of the African Bongo*') planned, by Cangary Films, to be shot in the Aberdare Mountains.

Charles remembered how cold and misty it was as the film took shape within the high altitude bamboo forests.

"Filming took several months, after which Margaret, Caroline and myself were invited, by the film company, to see 'rushes' of the film at Disney Studios, California. We took the opportunity for a much needed two-week vacation and a visit to Margaret's eldest son, Julian Sylvester, who owned his own company, Reptile Rentals, in California. We also took the opportunity to take Caroline to Disneyland, a memorable visit for all three of us.

"It became somewhat amusing when we met the film editors at Disney studios. After cutting and editing the *Bongo* film for so long, they felt they knew me personally as the white hunter Jock McEwan, the part I was playing, so they asked me, seriously, if I had 'bagged any elephants recently?' I thought they were 'taking the micky' but, turning to laugh with them I realized they were serious. In order not to embarrass them, or myself for that matter, I merely shrugged, before turning to one side, saying, 'Fraid not, old boy', which seemed to satisfy them.

"On our return to Kenya, life gradually became almost normal again with our fishermen members bringing in record-sized bass and tilapia for which prizes were given. Dances were held in the Clubhouse. Margaret's son Roger helped out in the bar when he was free from his travel bureau, usually at weekends, and everyone said how happy they were to have the place to themselves again.

"Michael, with promises of returning, left Kenya to attend Capetown University, South Africa, to study economics. I had a hollow feeling of loss again. Not only had I said goodbye, for a while, to my newly-found son, but also to a warm and understanding relationship."

In 1974, Screen Gems Film Company booked the Marina Club in order to begin the '*Born Free*' television series, an update on the original film of the same name, which had taken place almost 30 years previously.

Shortly after the television group arrived, the Kenya rains came down heavily, pouring through thatched roofs and flooding kitchens.

"One terrible lunchtime, I'm loath to recall," Charles grimaced, "the film company sat at their tables holding open umbrellas over their heads and, of course, wouldn't you believe it, Murphy's Law and all that, a huge country spider – harmless, but daunting to American city dwellers -- came in from the rain, hanging on its thick thread, as if transfixed, over the table of film star Gary Collins, who, with Dianna Muldaur as Joy Adamson in the television series, was to take the part of George Adamson. Nigel was amused by the spider's arrival, but others in the restaurant were not."

Luckily, weeks beforehand, when tourists, extra club members and the arrival of film makers made the cooking of many more meals essential, Charles was glad that the Bell Inn, in Naivasha township, less than five miles away, had been purchased by the LNE Company. Kitchens and staff there made life at the fully occupied Marina Club so much easier. Vans were sent each day to pick up extra food that was always needed.

"Within days," said Charles, "warm tropical rain still pouring, the Marina restaurant was swamped so that our large tents, for serving meals under cover outside, had to be taken out of storage and erected. Ironically the Marina radio kept blaring the tune of the time, 'Raindrops Keep Falling on my Head.' How we all hated that music!

Then there was a military coup in Uganda.

"Many of our club staff, being Ugandans, disappeared over the Kenya border to find their loved ones, some of whom, they were told, had been murdered. It was not a pleasant time for any of us. As for our company, Lake Naivasha Enterprises, with foodstuffs and housing material prices rising sky-high, there was little profit, but we soldiered on until the rain stopped.

"At the peak of the *Born Free Television Series*, on April 23rd, 1974, with divorces having been awarded us, I married my love, Margaret Ann, the mother of our daughter Caroline Rima.

"With the sweet perfume of coffee bushes in full bloom, and bougainvillea climbing at random in a profusion of pink and white blossoms spreading over hedgerows, we made our marriage vows in an African registrar's office in the little village of Kiambu, where we had first met that magic day ten years before.

"Witnesses at our wedding were our dear friends, white hunter John Lawrence and his wife Julia, two of Margaret's five children from her two previous marriages, Julian (Sylvester) --one of the reptile handlers and animal trainers for the *'Born Free'* TV series-- his sister Jane (Sylvester) and our little daughter Caroline. Roger (Sylvester) and Judy (Burke) were out of the country, as were my two children, Christine and Michael, from my first marriage, but we received warm and loving telegrams from them all which made us overjoyed by their acceptance of our new life together."

Within months the TV series, lock, stock and animals, packed up and left Kenya, moving back to the States followed by a Nairobi newspaper headline that read, ' A Million Dollar Flop'.

"With great happiness," said Charles, "we moved into Karuna House, which we had bought in Westlands, a suburb of Nairobi.

"Margaret and I drove the fifty miles to Naivasha frequently with our two hefty, Australian-made Holden cars filled to the gunnels with groceries and meat for our Lake Naivasha Marina Restaurant and the Bell Inn, both places which were doing well.

"I employed an African manager -- one of many managers during that time -- but soon the whole business of coping with the Marina, the lake waters receding, in its usual 30-year cycle (we were told), and its ever-going problems, became tiring. Also, Caroline had to attend school".

Much to his chagrin, the best school in Nairobi for Caroline was, at that time, a nearby Catholic school and as he didn't want to send her to England, a decision had to be made. A uniform was bought for her and she entered happily into Westland's Consolata Primary School.

A little difficulty arose at Christmas time when parents were invited to attend an evening service at the large and imposing Catholic Church. Caroline asked politely,

"Daddy, please come. There will be a lot of singing."

There was a deep breath, a split second's hesitation, then a smile and Caroline, her parents by her side, entered the church.

Opiyo, the family's mpishi, (cook), accompanied by one of his wives -- Opiyo wearing Charles' outgrown dinner jacket, Fred, the gardener, and his family, Lucy Nyambura, Caroline's Kikuyu ayah, (nanny-cum-housemaid), and a variety of African and European school friends of Caroline's all met at the church. With heady incense smoke surrounding them, small bells tinkling during the religious ceremony and colourful Christmas lighting, the Protestant Hayes' enjoyed together, as a new family, their first Catholic Church service.

English tourist Paul Osborne with Charles, showing Marina Club members the huge black bass caught in Lake Naivasha.

Charles , takes the part of a hunter, "In Search of the African Bongo", filmed in the Aberdare Mountains, Kenya.

Caroline with Charles during the family's visit to Disneyland, California.

The Bell Inn, Naivasha, gets a new roof.

Charles Hayes and Margaret Burke were married on April 23rd, 1974 at Kiambu, Kenya.

Margaret and Charles' 'Karuna House', Westlands, Nairobi, 1973.

TWENTY-THREE

Power and Lighting in East Africa

And the Sultan of Zanzibar said, "Let there be Light."

AT THE END OF 1975, the board of the East African Power and Lighting Company Limited, with offices based in Nairobi, wanted a book written on the Company's history to include the Tana River Development Company, The Kenya Power Company and the Mombasa Power and Lighting Company.

Contacted by Alan Ngugi, then secretary of the EAP&L, Charles was asked if he would write it. Always interested in history -- particularly African history -- Charles was delighted to sign an authorship contract, suggesting the book would probably take two to three years to complete.

Over the next few years, Charles gradually built up an informal history of the EAP&L, with his manuscript entitled, *Stima*, puzzling those who didn't know that it was the East African name for electricity.

When British naturalist Henry Hamilton Johnstone visited the Island of Cloves, (Zanzibar), in 1884, he found that wood-fired steam boilers generated electricity for the Sultan's Palace there. Africans called this new form of lighting, 'stima', from the English word 'steam', often pronounced 'sitima'. (Electric current was first generated in Nairobi by this method in 1908).

Johnstone, while in Zanzibar, wrote in his diary:

"As the shadows deepen, and the rose-tinted houses fade into dull grey, the stages of the Sultan's tower are picked out with yellow lamps, and suddenly from the sunset gleams out in cold

radiance a star of first magnitude -- Sultan Sayyid Barghash has fitted up his clock tower with electric light!".........

Research for the EAP&L book led Charles from archives in Kenya to the Thomas Edison Museum in Dearborn, Michigan, USA, a visit conveniently made while staying with his daughter Christine and her husband Alwyn Rougier-Chapman who lived in nearby Grand Rapids. It was a fine chance for Charles to meet grandsons Andrew and Duncan, to introduce Margaret to Christine, and Christine to her half-sister Caroline.

Shaking his head with more amusement than disbelief, Charles watched nine-year old Caroline play 'tag' with her new-found nephews, Andrew and Duncan, all three of them of similar age.

While vacationing at the Kenya Coast in 1978, Charles, working under the light of an oil lamp, moths and hundreds of harmless 'sausage' flies bumping about all over his desk and into his hair, completed the last chapter of the book *Stima*.

That night he wrote in his diary:

"Owls hoot from the fruiting baobab trees; dark bats swoop on their swift errands, their flight taking them across the plump moon, full as a yellow balloon rising above the edge of the sea. Insects surround the lamp in this room and the night is full of sound as my darlings sleep silently on and I write the closing words of a book which has become wearisome to me."

Next morning, the manuscript already on its way to Nairobi by Peugeot Express African taxi, the shocking news arrived that Kenya's President, Jomo Kenyatta, had died in his Coastal home in Mombasa, just miles away from where Charles and the family were staying.

The printing of the book, *Stima*, was therefore put on hold, but by the time Vice President Daniel Arap Moi, from the Elgeyo tribe, had been elected President of Kenya, the Hayes' family were making plans to emigrate to Canada, so it was not until several years later that Charles actually saw the printed copy of his book.

The book cover of *Stima*, 1979.

Charles' daughter Christine with husband
Alwyn Rougier-Chapman, at home in Michigan, 1997.

TWENTY-FOUR

From the Heart of a Tree

"I know that I shall never see a Poem as lovely as a tree."
Joyce Kilmer, 1888-1918

DURING THE FINAL MONTHS of writing his book, *Stima*, Charles was also in the process of putting together a 66-page glossy brochure on contemporary Makonde Sculpture for Madan Sapra, a collector of this type of art.

Sapra, who owned a photographic studio in Nairobi, had been collecting, for many years, rare Makonde sculptures bought from Tanzanians who carved them from the heart of African 'ebony' trees. Sapra had been invited by the Beverley Hills' Public Library and Auditorium in California to stage an exhibition of over 200 pieces of his African-ebony art collection.

By May that year the manuscript for the brochure was complete. With pages of superb black and white photographs of the Makonde art pieces, it was winging its way to the States for printing. A few days later Charles, Margaret and Caroline were also on their way to the US, via Air France, with a two-day stopover in Paris, where Charles, speaking in a mixture of Swahili and almost-forgotten French, told Caroline the history of Paris. They started at their hotel, within sight of the Arc de Triumph, and then by escalator to the top of the Eiffel Tower from where he pointed out places of historical interest.

By that time in his life, (aged 62), with legs that were not working as well as he would have liked, Charles was not keen on moving far on foot, so Caroline learned much about the French and their city without having to walk anywhere!

Over the next ten days Sapra's Makonde art exhibition, in Beverley Hills, became an astounding success. Film stars, including ZaZa Gabor, arrived for the opening cocktail party in clouds of perfume, wearing clothes that shouted 'Rodeo Drive'.

One large lady, a star from a well-known circus, did the splits while holding a glass of champagne, not spilling a drop. Charles grinned,

"This exhibition is becoming more interesting than I could have imagined."

Invited guests looked at each piece of sculpture, listened enraptured to Charles, who told them the history of the talented Tanzanians, then bought the huge Makonde sculptures for vast amounts of money. Everything was going well and, at the end of each tiring day, the Beverley Hills Hotel was a luxury to be enjoyed.

But, for the first time, Charles realized, during an embarrassing moment, that in the year 1977, smoking cigarettes was not an acceptable pastime in America.

While standing talking to guests at the Makonde exhibition, within the beautifully furnished Beverley Hills Library auditorium, he asked a well-coiffured assistant where he could find an ashtray. To his horror she absolutely screamed at him, "An ASH tray?" followed by turning to everyone in the room to say loudly,

"This gentleman wants an ASHtray," pointing, for effect, her long, scarlet-nailed finger at Charles, now the centre of a surprised group of Americans.

"Don't you realize sir, that smoking cigarettes is putting us ALL at risk for CANCER?"

If Charles had owned a tail he would have put it between his legs and crept away. He had never met such a brash-voiced woman; neither had he heard in Kenya that cigarettes, his happy lifetime habit, could possibly put any one's health in danger.

Looking her in the eye he said quietly, if not a little sarcastically, "I'm SO sorry madam." Bowing slightly he then opened the French windows to the library gardens, smoked a couple of his favourite Kenyan SM (sweet menthol) cigarettes, in order to calm himself, then stuffed ash and burnt-out stubs into his pocket.

At this point he should have burst into flames, but after two days of sneaking behind flowering garden shrubs to 'light up', he found that no-one would stand too near him because of his nicotine-impregnated suit, so it was sent to the cleaners and for the rest of the time in the States he kept hidden in his pocket, a small 'ash-tin', complete with a tightly fitting, screw-type lid.

CH enjoys a 'banned' cigarette on the grounds of the Beverly Hills Library, California.

A Makonde carving. (Pic: Madan Sapra)

"Botanically, there exists some 300 varieties of the so-called 'African ebony', a tropical tree, possibly now an endangered species, found south of the Sahara. The most commonly used by the Makonde artists is *Diosphyros mespiliformis* -- a rather stunted and deformed tree with a heartwood of dark brown to black which is heavy, hard and durable. It remains unaffected by termites and, when seasoned, rarely cracks. Many of the sculptures are seen to be pornographic. Others, some five feet tall or more, depict intricately carved family lives, from birth to grave."
From the American brochure, '*Contemporary Makonde Sculpture*' by Charles Hayes.

TWENTY-FIVE

Garden Party

*"I never expected to have, in my sixties,
the happiness that passed me in my twenties."*
C.S. Lewis

WITH THE NEWS that his son Michael had graduated from Capetown University and married, in South Africa, a charming journalist, Lynne Van Santen, Charles invited the couple to Kenya for their honeymoon.

Charles and Margaret organised a 'second' wedding reception held on the lawn of their house in Westlands, Nairobi. A string trio played while guests and family intermingled. It was Boxing Day December 1978 and the weather, as usual in Kenya, was at its hottest - perfect for a holiday at the Coast. Charles then admitted to having booked the family holiday house in the ancient village of Takaungu, between Mombasa and Malindi on the Kenya Coast, as a surprise so that the family could spend the first weeks of the New Year (1979) there together.

Charles explained that it was in the little village of Takaungu where the Danish Kenyan coffee farmer, Karen Blixen, had spent many romantic times with her lover, Denys Finch-Hatten. Blixen wrote several books, under the name of Isaac Dinnesen, including the world favourite, *Out of Africa*, which was later made into a best selling film.

Next morning the two large Holden cars were packed and, everyone singing loudly, with gusto, the whole Hayes family drove off to the Coast. It was a wonderful, never-to-be-forgotten family holiday.

Caroline, at 12 years old, was growing quickly and had moved up to the Loretto Convent School in Nairobi. Charles, worried at the number of protests by University students in Nairobi, where cars were turned over and burnt and shop windows smashed in, decided to look at other countries where his new family could live with less hassle. But he was quick to explain that it was not just the student situation.

"I am almost at the retirement age and would like to buy some land, build a house and write quietly for my own sake -- maybe publish books -- our own publishing company would suit us well."

By the end of Caroline's term, Charles had booked a three-month holiday, starting in Vancouver, Canada, with plans to travel through North America by comfortable Greyhound bus -- because he was not happy about learning, at that time, to drive 'on the other side of the road'.

"It's time we had a good look around. I have a cousin in British Columbia somewhere, although I haven't seen him for 50 years. We could try to find him."

That year, 1979, Charles, Margaret and young Caroline became aware of the Province of beautiful British Columbia, in a Canada they found more awe-inspiring than they had ever imagined.

Charles' cousin, John Braidwood, found by telephone while the Hayes' were staying in Vancouver, arranged to meet them in the holiday town of Penticton, 300 miles into the interior of BC.

"How shall I know him?" Charles worried.

But John Braidwood was the only person standing at the Greyhound bus terminal when they alighted.

Looking at each other Charles extended his hand towards his cousin. "Doctor Livingstone, I presume," said Charles, with a wide grin. From then on a long-awaited friendship was formed.

Taking trips through The States to look at pieces of land for sale, and meeting up with old friends, Charles decided to return to BC to look again at a 160 acre lot -- a quarter section, as it is known in

Canada -- that his cousin had taken Charles and Margaret to look at. The land consisted mainly of pine-wooded, rocky hilltops overlooking a small lake. It was beautiful but, it was pointed out, a well had to be drilled if anyone thought of living there.

Never daunted by a challenge, however difficult it may seem, Charles then got in touch with an old Norwegian water diviner, (in Canada called a 'water witcher') who, with witch hazel branch bending fit to bust in his hands, as it quivered earthwards, smiled, "plenty 'vawter' here!" As it turned out the witcher was absolutely correct. He had hit an artesian well.

Elated with the possibility of buying a little piece of Canada, Charles put a down payment on the land on Green Lake Road, Okanagan Falls, in British Columbia.

Within a week the Hayes' were on their way back to Kenya via Ireland, where they stayed first in a Tipperary bed and breakfast hotel before travelling on to friends in Dublin, where they drank Guinness in city pubs, (except 14-year-old Caroline), talked 'James Joyce' and other famous Irish writers and thoroughly enjoyed the Emerald Isle. Ireland's music, dancing and singing reminded Charles of his parents and their way of life when he was growing up.

One year later, having passed all health regulations in Kenya, property sold and taxes paid, the squeaky-clean Hayes family were welcomed into Canada as landed immigrants, settling happily on the piece of land they had fallen in love with, above the small town of Okanagan Falls, British Columbia.

House-building, well-drilling and furniture-buying took up most of their first year in Canada. The well gave as much water as was needed, giving more and more gallons per minute as the well 'settled down'.

Plans were made, tentatively, for travelling around Canada, but an urgent, open-heart operation stopped the family in their tracks when, in 1981, Charles was diagnosed with needing a new aortic valve.

The operation was performed successfully, shortly afterwards, at the Vancouver Hospital.

Jokes and cards, such as good wishes to, 'pig of my heart', arrived for him when it was found that he had had a new pig's valve inserted. As it turned out, it served him very well indeed, with no complications ever.

"Must have been a fine young pig," Charles commented, twenty years later.

Charles and Margaret's newly built "Maweni House" at Green Lake, Okanagan Falls, British Columbia. 1980.

Charles' son Michael marries Lynne Van Santen in Geneva, Switzerland, 1978.

Charles, Margaret and Caroline kiss the Blarney Stone during their holiday in Ireland, 1979.

TWENTY-SIX

Once an Editor, Always an Editor

"If you have an important point to make, don't try to be subtle or clever. Use a pile driver. Hit the point once. Then come back and hit it again. Then hit it a third time - a tremendous whack."
Winston Churchill

FEELING BETTER AND STRONGER, Charles began talking 'newspapers' again.

"What Okanagan Falls should have is a good country weekly," he grunted. (In fact, over the years, various people in the area had published small local newspapers, but never more than 4 to 8 pages at a time and none of the publications had lasted very long).

"With a paper that size, we could put it together before breakfast." (After time Charles regretted ever saying that).

With groans and moans from the family, and daily discussions underlining how nice it was that he could retire and enjoy Canada, Charles found that a small eight-pager newspaper, then being published in the Falls, was suddenly no more. The young editing couple had vanished one Friday night.

Elated beyond measure, Charles visited the local Credit Union to find that all the newspaper office furnishings -- a couple of desks, chairs and two old typewriters had been left behind and were for sale.

There was no stopping him. Suddenly -- and it was indeed suddenly -- a fellow from a real estate office arrived at the house with papers for him to sign. Charles had bought the large Variety Store, in the centre of Okanagan Falls, which, he said, was the perfect building ıaper office; but it would not be ready for another month or

ver-the-less, he insisted Margaret go with him to Castlegar, a town three and a half hours drive from Okanagan Falls, for there, he said, was a compugraphic typesetting machine he wanted her to see.

"It is for sale and it should be purchased now," he said firmly.

Of course Charles bought the cumbersome machine. Everyone knew he would. Rather like an old iron-framed piano, and incredibly heavy, the compugraphic came with two huge plastic containers of chemicals, 'developer' and 'fixer'. Like film, it would be needed for developing the typeset newspaper columns which would eventually, with luck, come churning out of the machine's mouth.

The whole lot was delivered to the Hayes' new house where a spare downstairs bedroom was converted into a newspaper office. "Goodbye retirement," Margaret sighed.

Neither Charles nor Margaret really knew how the beastly machine worked, "but we shall learn," said Hayes, the new editor of a weekly newspaper yet to be launched.

A few days later a charming woman knocked at the door.

"I am a typesetter trained on a compugraphic machine," she said, "I heard you were starting a newspaper and I would like a job."

She must have been more than surprised at the speed she was whisked inside the house and offered a position with a newspaper that Charles was still thinking about. But (Mrs.) Barbara Eby, from the nearby town of Oliver, had saved the day. She had a new job, the Hayes' sanity was intact and Charles' first problem was over.

Being Irish, and believing in 'the way of the leprechaun' of folklore fame, Charles was absolutely sure, he said, (with a twinkle in his eye), that the mischievous elf of the Emerald Isle had arranged things for him from the timing of his arrival in Canada at the precise moment a small newspaper had folded, to his finding a large building and a compugraphic typing machine 'up for sale' just when he needed it. The bonus of someone turning up at the right time, who knew how to use the machine, was leprechaun-planning for sure, begorra.

"You see, this newspaper is meant to be," said he, shrugging and smiling to himself.

With his tremendous interest in history, Charles was thrilled to talk to senior citizens in the Okanagan area and, in his charming manner, hear their stories, some of which had never before been heard or written. He searched out and bought old books on British Columbia, piecing together the pioneering of the Okanagan Valley, finding that the first newspaper published in the Falls, in 1893, was called the *Okanagan Mining Review*, which had lasted just eleven weeks.

Naming his new newspaper *The South Okanagan Review*, which he figured would take in advertising and stories from along the Valley, Charles hoped that his '*Review*' would last longer."

The first *South Okanagan Review* newspaper hit the streets the week of October 16th, 1982.

"A 52nd birthday celebration for Margaret," said Charles, pouring her a glass of champagne. Margaret rolled her eyes and set about, not very easily, learning how to develop, print and screen black and white photographs in a 'dark room'. Although a writer and photographer, she had never actually processed film or screened pictures herself, so there were many weeks when Review photographs were not of the best -- embarrassingly dreadful, she admitted -- but, with extra staff, things began to improve slowly.

In a double-column editorial named 'Viewpoint', the first week of publication, Charles wrote to his readers:

"A GOOD NEWSPAPER is a community talking to itself. It's people, the things they do and say. It's also the facts they require to know in order to make sound judgements and it's the opinions they form when they've had time to consider all points of view.

A good newspaper is a set of important signals, sent up by its readers, and it therefore deserves study by people in power. We wear no political label and we hope to avoid the platitudes of politics; but we shall appraise carefully what they're doing up there in the high places and if their actions have adverse effect upon the life of our community, we'll see if we can make them take notice.

In the South Okanagan, we believe, there exists a charm and an honesty of purpose rare in this world. The pulse of the people lies deep in our family units, which themselves interlock historically and in the economics of daily living. We pledge to do all we can to preserve a way of life that makes this area special. We'll try to keep track of those things which must be done for the needy and, where volunteers are already helping, we'd like to ensure that such kindliness does not go unnoticed.

Today, as we take our first step in South Okanagan publishing, we recognize our responsibilities and, with humility, we accept them. Both this newspaper, and the advertisers who support it, are here to serve its readers. To repeat then; a good newspaper is a community talking to itself. Let's hear from you neighbour."

In that first 8-page issue Charles also wrote about the *Okanagan Mining Review*, published ' just 89 years ago':

"WHY, we've been asked, do we call the South Okanagan's newest newspaper, the *Review*?

At the outset, let's confess to a sentimental regard for history. We find it thrilling to look back down the road to development and to visualize how things used to be around our first target area for distribution -- Kaleden and White Lake, Vaseux and Gallagher, Willowbrook (the former Meyer's Flat) and Okanagan Falls itself, all within about a 50-mile radius. And just 89 years ago, a newspaper was being published from Main Street, Okanagan Falls, designed to serve the newly developed "city" at the foot of Dog Lake -- today's Skaha Lake -- and the mining camps in what was referred to as "the Lower Country". It was known as the *Okanagan Mining Review* and the newspaper in your hands today is therefore something of a revival.

The first *Review* newspaper had been founded by two well-experienced journalists; George G. Henderson and "Major" Ainsley Megraw, of the *Vernon News* with which the *Mining Review* was associated.

The partners recruited an Ontario-born jobbing printer, Robert Matheson, as their "man in the Falls". In his hands, the little newspaper was homely and sprightly and informative, pawky in its humour and ready to lash out when it felt aggrieved.

The town site developer was W. J. Snodgrass, who had been successful in business in Oregon, USA, and was using his capital to make a dream come true -- his vision of a thriving metropolis set beside Dog Lake's blue waters.

It was planned to become the busy crossroads for water and rail communications, the centre of higher learning for the whole Okanagan Valley, the supply centre for what Snodgrass believed was the "greatest mining area in the world."

Something like a million dollars of placer-gold had already been taken out of the area between Rock Creek, the Similkameen and Mission Creek, in Central Okanagan.

Said the *Mining Review*, "Gold predominates, but silver, lead, copper, coal and platinum occur in extensive deposits, and 'Fairview'-- just up the road, the newspaper report went on, -- enjoys the distinction of being 'the first regular bullion-producing quartz camp in British Columbia.'

Fairview, of course, is not even a ghost town today. The coalmines of White Lake were worked only fitfully and finally closed in the 1930's. Much has changed, yet nothing changes. The first issue of the *Mining Review* -- eight pages, (just as we begin publication today), all in hand-set metal type -- contained more flagrant promotion material than the modern tourist agency or land developer would dare to use today, yet the thoughts expressed are still applicable.

One passage read:

'Judging by the large number of enquiries made regarding the Okanagan, it would appear that this district is attracting a number of home seekers. It would seem that the Okanagan has become the hope of those who are frozen out in other parts of the country.

Here the frozen will come to thaw out, while the rheumatic-jointed and weak-lunged will flock in to ease their tortures and prolong their days. As long as they bring plenty of cash with them, room will be found for their crutches and all allowance be made for their often infirmities.'"

That little newspaper lasted for only 11 issues, ceasing publication in the Falls in November, 1893.

In more recent times, other ventures have followed suit."

In that first issue of Charles' *South Okanagan Review*, in October 1982, advertisers helped pay Penticton's Moira Press printers.

There were half pages from the Falls Pharmacy, (then IDA), advertising fireworks. The Falls Hardware advertised everything from sweet apple cider to wrist watches, chain oil, stove pipe and chimney supplies. The OK Corral had for sale Western clothing, cowboy boots, belts and silver buckles and the Oliver Credit Union's headline on its half-pager was, "Salute to our Farm Industry." At the O.K. Food Mart, quality beef was selling hindquarters at $2.09 a lb. and the SunOka Inn, then at the bottom of Waterman's Hill leading to the bridge towards the Falls, was specializing, that week, their smorgasbord dinner, with Country Rock entertainment. Angie's Hairstyling was open five days a week, it was promised; the Oliver Cinema was showing E.T., and The Jade Shop, with Edna Bohn at the helm, advertised the sale of BC jade jewellery, ornaments and wooden carvings.

On page five, a double-column on cooking, written by Margaret, became a regular weekly feature in her 'Women's Eye View' pages.

In a short section, a veterinary surgeon noted that an unusual number of dogs were being peppered with porcupine quills.

A soon-favourite column was 'Willowbrook News', by Ethel Jones -- Willowbrook being a small enclave in the hills between Okanagan Falls and Oliver townships.

After the first issue of the *South Okanagan Review* tabloid there was never a shortage of top stories and news and, within a month or two, the weekly *Review* was being read from the city of Penticton and Naramata, south to Oliver and Osoyoos and in such faraway villages as Bridesville, Greenwood, Keremeos and Cawston, making a one-hundred-mile-round delivery trip through the Okanagan Valley.

Advertising was slow to start with, but the paper gathered momentum and was free to readers to begin with. Businesses watched carefully to see if 'this' newspaper would 'fold' within weeks, and began to trust it.

By 1983, two years later, paid subscriptions were suggested after 'freebie' copies were gradually discontinued.

Within weeks the *Review* print order had stepped up. Advertising sales staff members were busy and Rima Publication Ltd., the business name for the *Review*, was doing better than expected.

During his first years as editor/publisher of the *South Okanagan Review*, Charles made many friends and a few enemies. "That goes with the territory," he chuckled.

"You can't write, each week, the stuff every person wants to read."

Nevertheless, he earned respect from his readers. The letters' column told the story of who was reading the paper. Correspondence was either interested-intelligent, or angry-intelligent. Nevertheless, both types of reader went on subscribing, he noted, which to Charles' delight, kept opinions flowing.

"This is like Wimbledon," he was heard to say, as letters sped backwards and forwards after a particularly debatable piece had been published.

In 1983, Charles was asked by the President of the Okanagan Falls Women's' Institute, if he would help bid for a very special building known locally as 'Bassett House', which was due to come under the auctioneer's gavel.

The house, along with many old artefacts donated by local residents, had been protected for several years at a site known as "Mystery Village", and now the house was to be moved to make way for modern housing development.

It was also feared that this rare piece of Falls' history was in danger of being lost.

The old wooden house had been the first pre-fabricated building in the Falls, shipped in parts by rail, stern wheel and horse-drawn cart. It had been ordered from a T. Eaton and Company catalogue in 1906 and constructed in Okanagan Falls by the Bassett Brothers, well-known kings of the old-time stagecoach and freighter lines. The house had stood beside Shuttleworth Creek, in the centre of the Falls, ever since.

The local Kiwanis Club stepped in with offers to help buy the old dwelling, but when members of the Women's Institute heard that someone from Alberta was coming to the auction, to bid for their house, they were adamant they didn't want it to be taken to another Province. After all, they said, the house had been the residence of

Margaret Bassett, the former Miss McLelland, daughter of the Falls' first postmaster, John McLelland.

Charles, who enjoyed auctions at any time, said certainly he would do their bidding for the old house.

The Women's Institute had $5,000 to play with, they told him, but hoped, of course, the house could be bought for less.

On the day of the auction Charles was ready, sitting in a strategic place where he could see who was the out-of-town stranger he was to bid against. It didn't take long to figure out. Only the two men played along up to the $2,000 mark. Then Charles, thinking the stranger was bidding too high too quickly, remembered what he had heard during his first weeks in Canada when a shouting match between two Canadian loggers had amused him. Seeing the anxious faces of the WI members, he took courage.

Walking up to the 'stranger' he pulled himself up to his full 6-feet, saying quietly,

"If you don't stop bidding NOW, I shall break yer knees."

The bidding stopped. The stranger got out of his seat and left. Charles, the final bidder for this important item for the Falls, then bought the house for $2,500.

The next problem was where to move it.

The *South Okanagan Review* was filled with letters and news for weeks to come as Charles cajoled and wrote to members of the community asking if anyone had a piece of land, preferably in the Falls' area, they would consider selling. His efforts paid off and with offers of a six-month, no-interest loan by Falls' vintner, Albert le Comte, a piece of land, very close to the old Mystery Village, on Highway 97, was purchased.

The day of the house move was a spectacular event.

With police guard and road service, Charles was out on the highway at 3 a.m., the quietest time of night, camera in hand, watching under brilliant lighting the procedure of the old house being craned carefully onto a flatbed truck and moved very slowly across the Falls' bridge to its new resting place just metres away.

"That was a tricky move," Charles was heard to say the next day, "there were only a few inches to spare on either side of the bridge."

In 1982, Margaret's eldest daughter, (Mrs.) Janey Bell, was suddenly widowed. Her husband, Basil Bell, had died of a heart attack in Kenya, where they lived. Left with a ten-month-old son, (Oliver), Charles suggested that if Jane wanted to move to Canada she would be an asset to the *South Okanagan Review*.

As office manager for FAO, (Food and Agricultural Organisation), Nairobi, for several years, Janey was an expert typist and organizer.

In April 1983, Janey Bell left Kenya with her young son, one night, in the middle of a sudden, unexpected coup. Bullets were flying overhead and cars being turned over. Her plane was the last to leave Nairobi airport for several days and they arrived in Canada safely.

Janey's skills as office organizer and typesetter made all the difference to life at the *Review*, especially as she had arrived at a time when Barbara Eby, who had run the office compugraphic machine perfectly since her arrival, had broken her arm!

At this point it was suggested that Margaret's second daughter, artist Judith Burke, might like to join the *South Okanagan Review* team but after a holiday with the family in British Columbia she married her love, Niccolo Roselli-Cecconi. They started a picture framing company and art gallery in Johannesberg, South Africa. In 2000, with their two sons Filippo and Mikele, they made their home, where Niccolo had been born, in Tuscany, Italy.

A year and a half later, on the 29th December 1984, during the heaviest snowfall in years, Janey Bell married Canadian Bruce Volden at St. Saviour's Chapel, Penticton, Charles escorting his stepdaughter down the aisle. A son, Casey Duff Volden, was born in 1985.

The years of newspaper publishing rolled on. Charles had promised that after five years he would sell the business and take the family for a lengthy look at the rest of Canada. But buyers came and went, Charles disliking most of them, not always personally, but hating the fact that most of them were not well enough experienced in writing, let alone the editing of a newspaper. One possible buyer hadn't enough money and had the cheek to ask if Charles would lend it to him!

"They are not having our newspaper," growled Charles, adding under his breath, "pontificating pisspots."

In January 1985, Charles' wrote in his weekly 'Viewpoint' column:

"IT WAS ONCE SUGGESTED that a magazine should be published containing nothing but letters from readers. They could then 'ride hobby-horse and argue with one another without anybody interfering,' noted Bernard Levin, distinguished columnist and drama critic of *The Times*, of London, England.

The old maxim was that for every letter written and published there were another thousand people who agreed with those views but had been pipped at the post by not having themselves taken up pen and paper sooner.

In recent weeks we, at *Review*, have been purring a little as subscriptions poured in by mail. Many of such letters included the most charming notes, explaining why each subscriber wanted *Review* delivered to him (or her, or them) by mail regularly every week.

It would have been tempting to publish such comments; but modesty rightly prevailed -- even though we were delighted to learn from this harvest of comment what our readers want from us. You have told us the 'editorial mix' is right; that you like the choice of *Review* features; that you find yourselves reading this newspaper 'as if it were a letter from a friend'.

There's an affectionate bond between us, you've said, and you peruse *Review* 'from cover to cover'. You've appreciated the newspaper coming to you free during the years since it was established, you've said, and you understood that the time for subscription had now arrived. We've also had the chance of meeting the hundreds of readers who preferred to call in with their subscriptions and told us that the philosophy on which this publication was established -- the bringing together of our near communities -- was correct. You have remarkably wide interests and you want background to news events, analysis in depth; but you're not concerned to know every detail about people making the news.

Thank you all for the warmth of your welcome. As we grow further, in the years to come, we'll keep faith."

Charles was overworking, spending hours during the day, and sometimes long into the night, writing, re–writing and updating articles and last minute news items.

During the day many people came to visit him in the office, usually at the busiest times, wanting to tell him stories, to 'just sit and talk', or bring in advertising. At moments like these he would plead,

"I'm only the editor; please talk to Margaret or Jane." And so he would get some time to concentrate.

'I'm only the editor' became such a joke with the *Review* staff that they bought him a coffee mug with the phrase printed clearly around it.

After Caroline Rima Hayes graduated from South Okanagan Senior Secondary school, in Oliver BC, she achieved a Business Administrative diploma from Okanagan College, Kelowna, prior to completing a two-year business program at Simon Fraser University in

Vancouver. She also attended evening classes in Certified General Accounting at the University of British Columbia. But it was not long before she fell in love with the man she would marry.

With great pride, on October 10th, 1987, Charles led his lovely young daughter, Caroline Rima, down the aisle in St. Saviour's Church, Penticton, to present her to Bradney Roy Webb. A wedding reception was held for the young married couple at Penticton's Delta Lakeside Resort.

The following year, Brad and Caroline presented Margaret and Charles with a grandson, Brook Eugene Webb. A granddaughter, Aimee Marie Helena Webb, sister for Brook, was born on March 31st, 1991.

Charles and his daughter Caroline Rima enjoy a quiet moment before escorting her down the aisle.

Bradney Roy Webb marries Caroline Rima Hayes at St. Saviour's Church, Penticton, British Columbia, October 10th, 1987.

Charles with grandson Brook Webb in 1990. Grandaughter Aimee at the age of 3 in 1994.

At the end of 1989, Charles, who had been having trouble with his legs, underwent a right hip replacement. After a successful operation in Penticton Hospital, he was advised not to cross his legs for at least six weeks. After eight days, he was sent home. Happy to be back at his office desk he promptly crossed his legs! An ambulance was called for, and in great pain, Charles was once more in hospital having his hip popped back into place.

In October, 1990, the *South Okanagan Review* headline read, "Now we are Eight -- A Souvenir Issue." On page four, Charles wrote an editorial celebrating eight years of publishing in Canada, repeating his original pledge, "to do all we can to preserve a way of life which makes this area special," adding, "we'd like the *South Okanagan Review* to make its way towards the homes of modern readers for a good long time to come."

That year many interesting letters from local readers came fast, some furious, to the *Review,* during the time when the possibility of Okanagan Falls being incorporated was being discussed.

'Town Pump' meetings were disrupted, tempers flared, chairmen walked out and residents of the Falls, for a while, were divided. Then everything subsided. The Falls never did incorporate, (at least it hadn't by year 2003).

The *South Okanagan Review* staff dressed in the 1800's style for the 1982 Christmas edition. Back row: Merida Cumming, Advertising Rep, Caroline Hayes, Typesetter, Charles Hayes, Editor, Margaret Hayes, President of Rima Publications Ltd.

On October 9, 1987, Charles surrendered his Kenyan citizenship to become a fully-fledged Canadian.

Fred King, MP for the Okanagan Similkameen, welcomes the Prime Minister of Canada, Brian Mulroney, to British Columbia where he was introduced to Charles Hayes, Editor of the *South Okanagan Review*. Penticton, 1987.

TWENTY-SEVEN

Into the Nineties

"When genuine passion moves you,
say what you've got to say, and say it hot."
D.H.Lawrence

IN ONE 1990 ISSUE of the *South Okanagan Review*, Charles' weekly editorial was headed, 'What is the Alternative', writing about the new British Columbia budget soon to be broadcast:

"THE SIGNS SUGGEST that provincial government purse strings will be seen to be drawn tight when finance minister Mel Couvelier's budget is revealed next week. He's expected to freeze wage demands and corral the expenditure mavericks. And, before anyone starts up the agony wail, it may be good to put the question once more, what's the alternative?

The buzzwords in BC's political Victoria, these days, are 'fragile prosperity'. A clever catch phrase because it's so prophetically evident that things ain't what they might have been. Opposition challenges notwithstanding, the calls for lavish spending being what they are -- election-wooing songs, most everyone appreciates straight talking. If the case for curbs on provincial ministries is proven, nobody will be surprised. It takes political courage, but it has to come".

Charles went on…. "From the Ottawa dog fight came some transparent comment this week as Opposition parties pitted their vocalists and spear throwing at Michael Wilson's new tax.

According to MP Jack Whittaker's newsletter, New Democrat leader Audrey McLaughlin 'regretted the Liberal refusal to offer any alternatives to the GST.'

Said McLaughlin, "They say their job is to simply oppose anything the Government does. That's not good enough. Canadians deserve an honest and open approach to tax policy."

Now, with those winsome words ringing in our ears, what exactly is the 'open and honest' alternative? Merely to go for the corporation jugular, as the NDP continually suggests?

C'mon. You can do better than that Audrey. We cannot toboggan comfortably downhill all the time without climbing the slopes to the top from time to time. Let's take the strain and pull on the rope, together."

At the age of 78, Charles' health was seen to be wavering. He was diagnosed with diabetes.

"Welcome to the club," said Okanagan Falls' doctor, James Robertson, after receiving tests back from the hospital, adding that there were thousands of people in British Columbia who were suffering from Type 2 diabetes.

It was suggested that Charles cut down his heavy smoking habit, which of course he didn't. Life in the newspaper business eased up considerably when the original large *Review* office was sold and a newly built, smaller and more comfortable place was purchased further along the Falls' Main street.

New computers were purchased, the old compugraphic typesetting machines given to boat owners as hefty anchors and Charles and Jane set to work learning the new, and far easier, way of typesetting. They found the whole procedure superbly efficient and life for everyone at the *Review* office was 'looking up'.

"A weekly newspaper allows readers to think about what they have read," said Charles, "to receive and perceive news, and the births, marriages and deaths column ('hatches, matches and dispatches') is an important way, as in all papers, of giving neighbours, especially in a spread-out community, news of their friends and acquaintances."

In 1993, a plea came from friends Juni and Hans Zwager for Charles to write the history of the Djinn Palace, their home on Lake Naivasha in Kenya. Charles' company had sold 'Oserian' to the Zwagers in 1968.

It was too good a challenge for him. Almost immediately Charles was in touch with old-time editor of the *Penticton Herald*, Phil Stannard, who was very happy to edit the *South Okanagan Review* for the few months the Hayes' would be in east Africa.

Phil had run a small Falls weekly which he had sold before the Hayes' had arrived in BC, so was familiar with the people in the area.

Well overdue for a holiday, the Hayes' spent their first two weeks in Provence, France, where Charles' son Michael and his wife Lynne owned a home. It proved a great time for getting to know grandchildren, Tara-Leigh, Guy and Dominic.

On one happy occasion, Charles, to the delight of the family, added to his grandchildren's evening of show-time acting and singing, by giving a stand-up rendition of an old London song. Donning a checked cap he sang, in a cockney accent, '*The Barrer's (barrow's) in the Walworth road*'. A few of the words went like this;

> '*You can buy half-a-dozen eggs, or a pair of wooden legs*
> *off the barrer's in the Walworf Road,*
> *You can get yer pockets picked, or get your whats'it kicked*
> *near the barrer's in the Walworf Road.*'

He even went so far as to do a little tap dancing to accompany his song!

In Kenya research needed for the book Charles was to write took the main part of their leave, although many days were spent with the Zwagers on exciting safaris and game viewing. "With time running out

- we had to return to Canada fairly soon -- it was decided that the Oserian history would have to be continued after our return home in February 1994."

The flight homewards took Charles and Margaret to Singapore where they stayed at the Regent Hotel, and dined at the prestigious Tanglins Club, (associated with Kenya's Muthaiga Club).

They found Singapore to be a flower-filled city with little or no crime, wishing they had more days to spend there.

Hong Kong was their next stopover, staying at the Excelsior Hotel, Hong Kong Island, for a few days shopping and sightseeing. They were particularly impressed by a tour to Hong Kong's tallest mountain, Tai Mo Shan, from where they could view 'The Land Between'. Commonly known as the 'New Territories', it is the land between Hong Kong and China, which they could see in the far distance.

Each day on the waterfront causeway, opposite the Excelsior Hotel, the Noon-Day six-pounder gun was fired, a tradition dating back to 1842 in the earliest days of Hong Kong's establishment as a British Colony.

The land on which the gun now stands was bought from the British Government by a trading company with plans to build on it.

A battery of guns was set up in order to protect the site from marauding Chinese sea pirates, but it also became the custom for the company to fire a multi-gun salute to signify the arrival or departure of a company chief executive, or taipan. However, this salute caused considerable annoyance to the resident Senior Naval Officer, so the company was officially reprimanded by the British Colonial Office and was ordered, as a penance, to fire just one gun at noon everyday to act as a time signal for the Colony.

Except for the period during the Second World War, the Noon-Day Gun has been fired as regularly as clockwork everyday since.

Charles and Margaret, enjoying a drink at the hotel's Noon-Day Gun bar, looked down to the causeway below, fascinated by the precision and timing of the daily routine. Charles remembered, and sang quietly, the words of Noel Coward, "In Hong Kong they strike a gong, and fire off a Noon Day gun, but mad dogs and Englishmen go out in the midday sun." In 1968 Noel Coward, on a visit to Hong Kong, was invited to fire the Noon-Day gun which, it was reported, he did with great aplomb.

In May 1995 the Rotary Club of Penticton joined with the Okanagan Falls' Chamber of Commerce to present Charles with the Citizen of the Year award which read:

'In recognition and appreciation for many years of dedication to our community.'

Charles was then 80 years old.

The stress of writing the book on Kenya, running the *Review* newspaper and staying up all night before publication each week to ensure latest stories appeared on the front page, 'Last Night in the Valley', left Charles exhausted. But he still spent weekends ghostwriting books for friends.

In their early days in Canada, Charles and Margaret had registered the companies, Rima Publications Ltd., and Rima Books, which worked well both for the publication of the *Review* newspaper and for any books they hoped to write.

That first year, Charles had worked with Victor and Joan Casorso of Oliver, BC, on their book, *The Casorso Story*, a special celebration of the Italian Casorso family's 100 years in British Columbia. Subsequently, other writers sought Charles' assistance, so by 1995, when Charles was well into his 80th year, Rima Publications *Ltd.* had produced six books, including *The Casorso Story*, (Victor Casorso), *The Countryman*, (FergusMurphy), *Okanagan Orchardist*, (Bert Hall), *Where the Tarmac Ends,* (Margaret Hayes), *The Review Cookbook and Prose*, (Margaret Hayes) and *The Story of the Okanagan Game Farm: From Rabbits to Rhino's, Gophers to Gnus*, (Pat Hines).

Charles, all the while, was working on his own book, *Okanagan Odyssey*, which he thought would be published, most probably, in two volumes. He knew it would take him several years to accomplish, mainly because it would entail weeks of travelling through the Okanagan Valley in Canada to the 'Okanogan', (spelt with an 'o' in it), Valley in Washington State, (over the border, 'next door'), to dig out history and to interview some of the pioneers who still lived there. Other books were more urgently needed, so *Okanagan Odyssey* was put on hold until such time it could be completed.

Charles with grandson Dominic. 1999.

At Sentosa, the Isle of Tranquility, Singapore. 1997.

Charles at a religious centre in Hong Kong. 1997.

TWENTY- EIGHT

Time to Move On

"I'm glad you like adverbs - I adore them;
they are the only qualifications I really much respect."
Henry James, 1912

THE DAY Charles and Margaret had looked forward to, especially since 81-year-old Charles was not then in the best of health, arrived in 1996 when David Obee, a newspaper editor, who had spent some 23 years with major newspapers in the Okanagan and in Alberta, and his wife Dixie, arrived from Calgary hoping to buy the *South Okanagan Review* newspaper.

Charles approved of David Obee, knowing instinctively the *Review* newspaper would be in professional hands, so the sale was completed fairly quickly.

On January 25th, 1996, Charles wrote his last piece as editor for his newspaper.

Headed, 1t's Time to Retire', he thumbed through memories of the *South Okanagan Review* saying:

"THIS ISSUE is the last for which Margaret and Charles Hayes are responsible." He went on, "taking over as new owners, from February 1st, are well-experienced journalist Dave Obee and his wife Dixie.

Established in 1982, with the prime object of serving Okanagan Falls' readers, *Review* quickly took on the role of a country newspaper, bringing South Okanagan communities together, to share views and compare progress. Peering back along those fourteen years of publishing is a pleasurable experience, particularly because of the many friendships made along the way and the trust shown us by the people of this very special Valley.

At the outset, we said, "A good newspaper is people, (a community), talking to each other, and sometimes comment has been raw. Free of any political label, *Review* has carried many differing points of view, so that readers may consider them and make informed judgments. For us, the results have been doubly rewarding for the opinions which readers express about the direction in which this country is heading are significant and worth study by our leaders.

Next week, Davis Obee will outline the future of *Review* and he'll give this newspaper a new look; refreshing vigour.

We shall still be around to assist and, in the days to come, we look forward to meeting all of you whose friendships we value. *Margaret and Charles Hayes.*"

With much of the book on Kenya having been completed, arrangements were soon made for Charles and Margaret to spend again some time in Kenya so that the commissioned book, entitled *Oserian, Place of Peace -- a Century of the Kenya Story*, published by Rima Publications Kenya Ltd., could be printed by Kenya Litho, Nairobi.

Oserian, the long-awaited book that had taken Charles nearly five years to write, was ready for sale by mid December 1996, offering the Hayes' and the Zwager's a relieved Christmas season at the Djinn Palace where, on Christmas afternoon, an African choir sang carols on the lawn and a huge, decorated tree held gifts for everyone.

The new year was celebrated by flying in the Zwager's private King Air plane, soaring through puffy, cotton-wool clouds well above snowy-topped Mount Kenya and landing smoothly a half-hour later on

Larson's luxurious Safari Camp runway set near the Uwaso Nyero River, (now spelt Ewasu Nyero) in Kenya's Samburu country.

While guests drank champagne, crocodiles lay on the opposite muddy bank smiling toothily at the sun, monkeys pelted everyone in sight with hard fruits snatched from doum-palm trees and hippos snorted and puffed in the earth-red water.

During the last hour of the old year, African Samburu dancers thrilled everyone as they whirled in the red dust under a full moon's pastel light, singing high-pitched tribal songs from long ago. Heavily-beaded necklaces bounced up and down on their necks as they jumped in time to the rhythm of the dance.

Nearby, orange flames from a crackling bonfire threw interesting shadows as the dancers, on the stroke of midnight, banged drums and blew whistles to welcome in 1997.

Yet, not too far away, the sound of hyenas, singing in their unique, up-scale voices, an occasional roar from a lion, and elephants trumpeting their irritation at the new-year cacophony, could be heard clearly. It was a night of pure African magic.

Later that month Juni Zwager organised a large garden party at her home, the Djinn Palace, (Oserian), on the shores of Lake Naivasha, where over two hundred guests, many of them well-known friends, came to talk to Charles and buy the books he signed. A second book signing took place early February at the famous old Norfolk Hotel in Nairobi for people who had been unable to travel upcountry.

Before leaving Kenya, another memorable safari was enjoyed when the Zwager's pilot flew the Hayes' over a clear, turquoise sea to Zanzibar -- the Island of Cloves -- just over the border into Tanzania where they all stayed in an 'old fashioned' thatch-roofed hotel built above a silvery, sandy beach scattered with tiny white shells. Unlike the new air conditioned coastal hotels, which tourism demands, it was a place where happy memories of family holidays at the Kenya Coast were recalled, encouraged, no doubt, by the almost overpowering sweet scent of ripening mangoes and over-ripe cashew-nut fruits. No doubt the quantities of ice-cold beer to drink also helped everyone's memory of 'old times'.

Charles and Hans Zwager celebrate the new year and the completion of the Zwager's book, *Oserian*, 1997, at Larson's Safari Camp, Kenya.

Charles' last safari to Kenya; happy to see Paulo, one of the members of his original house staff. December, 1996.

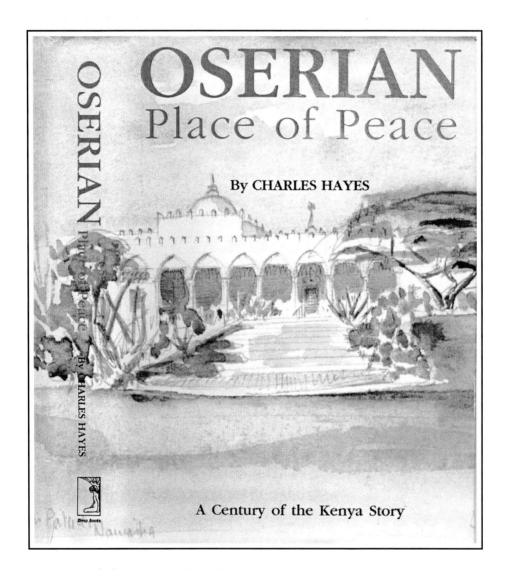

Signing his new book, *Oserian* at the Palace on Lake Naivasha. 1997.

Before visiting Zanzibar's famous Stone Town, they had to buy a tank of 'black market' fuel for the hired African driver. The matatu (taxi-bus) fuel was syphoned from a rusty barrel in a grubby back street as there was little or no petrol to be bought legally in Zanzibar.

The house of the late explorer Doctor David Livingstone was located, still in fairly good condition, on the sea front. Also facing the sea, the Sultan of Zanzibar's Palace, shelled by the British Navy in August 1896 in order to evict an illegal relative posing as the claimant, was now under more construction. A century before, the shelling of the Palace lasted less than 45 minutes and is recorded as the shortest war in history. Now known as the 'House of Wonders', the original palace, built by Sultan Seyyid Barghash in the 1880's, was the first building in eastern Africa to produce electric light by steam engine, (tinga-tinga ya sitima). A newer palace stands nearby.

Zanzibar was a town of contrasts with its magnificent carved doors, its smelly passageways where beautiful little children play around open drains and live lobsters squirm on door steps amongst bunches of bananas. Woven baskets filled with over-ripe mangoes ooze juice, while scraggy chickens skritch and scratch a living from rubbish found on the street. When it was time to return to Nairobi the pilot was told there was no aviation fuel on the island.

With a moment or two of panic all round, and a quick check in the fuel tank, the pilot decided it was risky, but there might just be enough to reach Nairobi. Luckily, there was.

Finally, on their way back to Canada via London, the Hayes' attended another *Oserian* book-signing party arranged at Rothschild Mews in the home of Karl Zeigler and his partner Jane. Karl had taken many of the coloured photographs for the book.

While in London, Charles took Margaret on a 'memory lane' boat trip down the Thames to Greenwich from Westminster Pier, passing the Tower of London and the many other historical places along the river. At Greenwich they lunched in an old English pub and looked over the famous 'Cutty Sark'. Built in 1869, it was the last ship used in the Chinese tea trade, and was standing in all its glory, in new polish and paint, on dry land.

The following day Charles, with his son Michael, (whose office was in the city), met Charles' cousin, Audrey Clarvis. Her husband Ted had arranged a special luncheon for them at Lloyds of London, the insurance market unique in the world.

Ted, who had been a broker and director with the company for 43 years, (an underwriting member for 25 years), gave the Hayes' the grand tour of Lloyds and a shortened history of the time when, in 1688, Edward Lloyd had opened a coffee house. Lloyd, it is said, 'encouraged a clientele of ship's captains, ship owners and merchants with an interest in overseas trade'.

Charles and Michael in London, 1997.

Edward Lloyd gained a reputation in trustworthy shipping news and Lloyd's coffee house became the recognised place for obtaining marine, and later, air insurance. The loss of RMS Titanic was entered in the casualty book at Lloyds in 1912. In 1988, Lloyd's celebrated its tercentenary. Edward Lloyd could never have foreseen how his humble coffee-drinking establishment would one day be transformed into the world's most remarkable entrepreneurial insurance market.

Back in the city, shortly before travelling back to Canada, there were tears in Charles' eyes as he stood on London Bridge, remembering how he used to run across it in the years of his youth and knowing, almost for certain, that he would never see London again.

Six months' of research, hard work, holiday and partying in the two countries they knew so well, gave Charles and Margaret the zest they needed for their retirement at home in Canada.

But, before long, another book was in the offing.

The family of a pioneer who had become a 'lumber baron' in British Columbia asked Charles if he would write their history.

"I would be delighted," said Charles, and so a busy retirement was off to a fine start.

Realizing that his own, partly-written book on the Okanagan would have to be put on hold again, he began at once the research needed for the new book by inviting to his house as many of the Leir family members he could 'round up'. With a glass of wine in their hands the Leir family started talking together, discussing their past. Charles listened and recorded stories that, the Leirs' admitted, had almost been forgotten over the years.

During 1999, Charles experienced several small strokes and was hospitalized three times.

With his blood circulation not working as it should, his toes became gangrenous and blackened and he was in so much pain that one surgeon suggested taking off his legs.

Charles, for the second time in his life said, "You will not lop them off." But a clever vascular surgeon, Dr. Bob Ellett, who worked an hour away at the Kelowna hospital, was the kindest and most understanding, telling Charles that he was not in the business of removing legs but would try to save them by operating just on his toes. Charles' agreed and his feet healed well.

Thankful, and much relieved, he told Dr. Ellett that he had never liked his toes anyway!

Healthwise, it was a bad two years for Charles. Nevertheless, by Christmas week 1999 Charles, then in a wheel chair, sat for four hours at Penticton's 'Leir House of the Arts' signing copies of *Hugh Leir—the Remarkable Enigma*, the book that he had completed with the help of daughters Caroline Webb and Janey Volden.

"Well," he was heard to say that day, "I haven't lost my legs and I believe I have not yet lost my marbles, so let's get on with some more writing. A Merry Christmas everyone!"

By March 18th, 2000, nearby members of the Hayes' family and close friends celebrated Charles' 85th birthday at home at Maweni House, Okanagan Falls.

It was a happy weekend party at which fifty or more people 'dropped in' each afternoon to wish him well. Charles' friend Paul Hariton, along with his wife Patti, drove down from the neighbouring town of Kelowna and, because the day before was St. Patrick's Day, Paul sang some of Charles' favourite Irish songs in his splendid rich voice. There wasn't a dry eye in the house.

Less than a month later Charles was, yet again, taken to hospital. After a short while he regained consciousness enough to enjoy a lively discussion with Margaret.

Later that day, on April 14th, after kissing him goodbye, Margaret told him she would come to drive him home next morning.

But Charles died peacefully in his sleep in the late afternoon.

++++++++++++++++++++++++++++++++++++

After cremation, as were his wishes, Charles' ashes were scattered in his garden beneath a flowering Catalpa tree by close members of the family.

Anecdotes and memories were remembered by his son, Michael, and youngest daughter, Caroline (Webb). Grandson Brook (Webb), read the Boy Scout's Law and promises from a book by Lord Baden Powell. Charles' step-grandson, Oliver Bell-Volden, recently returned from Tanzania, read messages from family members who were unable to attend the memorial. Charles' daughter Christine, with her son Andrew Rougier-Chapman, added happy memories, as did Margaret and her sons, Julian (USA) and Roger Sylvester (Kenya).

A short service and prayers were read by Pastor Jim McNaughton.

Near the house, within sight of Green Lake, which Charles said he never wanted to leave, a bronze plaque, set on the side of a large natural rock, bears the message in the English/Kiswahili languages:

> Charles Arthur Andrew Hayes. 1915-2000
> Respected author, journalist and gentleman.
>
> *(Dum diama Mlele Mlele Akae peponi na Maweni)*
> Alive for ever and ever with
> soft winds amongst the rocks.

Charles, happy at home in Okanagan Falls, B.C., Canada. 1999.

Letter of Condolence

A large company of people in Canada, Europe and Africa will be saddened by the news of the death of Charles Hayes, former editor of the South Okanagan Review. And they will be saddened for many reasons, but chiefly because he was an affirmative, outgoing, civilized human in their community. Others will write of his fine contributions in Africa and Europe, but a large company here will join his wife, Margaret, in both thanksgiving and sorrow.

A distinguished Scotsman, John Buchan, who became Canada's governor general, before he died wrote an account of his own life, and to that account gave the title 'Memory Holds the Door'. For Margaret, and the people who were warmed, cheered, and vitalized, memory now holds the door to a dear friend, Charles.

In the coming weeks many will make written tributes to one whose skilful pen touched the life and community with gentleness, charity and wisdom.

J..Alan Jackson, The Venerable Archdeacon,
British Columbia. Canada.

Family Album

Photographing butterflies at Sokoke Forest, Kilifi, Kenya Coast. 1968.

Charles chairs a meeting in Kenya. 1968.

Lake Naivasha. 1972.

Charles and Margaret Hayes in California. 1987.

British Columbia. 1992.

The Sons:

Margaret's sons Roger & Julian Sylvester and Charles' son Michael.

The Daughters:

Caroline, Janey, Judi and Chris.
At the Hayes family reunion, Okanagan Falls, BC. 1993.

Charles' son Michael with his wife Lynne and their three children Tara-Leigh, Guy and Dominic (right). London, England, 1997.

Charles with daughters Christine and Caroline. 1997.

'Maweni House', B.C. 1998.

1998.

Charles with his son Michael at Big White Ski Resort.
Kelowna, Canada,1999.

Christine and her husband Alwyn Rougier-Chapman with their sons Andrew (left) and Duncan, May 9, 1998.

The marriage of Charles' grandson: Dr. Duncan Peter
Rougier-Chapman to Elissa Margaret (Maggie) Scurry,
May 9, 1998, in Charleston, S. Carolina.

Julian and Sue Sylvester with their sons Justin (left) and Jonathan.
California, 2001.

Niccolo and Judi Roselli-Cecconi with their sons Filippo and Mikele.
At home in Tuscany, Italy. 2001.

Laura and Roger Sylvester with daughters Shana and Victoria.
Kenya, 2003.

Janey and Bruce Volden with their sons Oliver and Casey.
Okanagan Falls, BC, Canada. 2003.

Christine Rougier-Chapman, 2003.

Caroline and Brad Webb with their children Aimee and Brook.
British Columbia, Canada. July, 2003.

Caroline Rima Webb. 2003.

 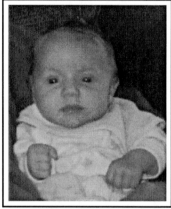

Charles' great-grandchildren Connor and Samantha Rougier-Chapman.

Acknowledgments

My grateful thanks to Gerry Loughran, who was the Assistant Editor of the *Sunday Nation*, Kenya, 1960-64, (later a Foreign Correspondent and Foreign Editor of *United Press International*), for his sensitive editing of this book. Although he is now a retired journalist, Gerry continues to write, from England, his '*Letter from London*' regularly for the *Sunday Nation*.

To my dear friend Julia Lawrence, (Kenya), who with her special sense of humour, has 'put me right' when memory failed, and her son Tom Lawrence, who spent time researching archives on wartime Burma, my love and appreciation. For the amazing safaris 'down memory lane' that my long-time friend Juni, and her husband Hans Zwager, arranged during my last visit to Kenya, I remain overwhelmed at their generosity. For teaching me the workings of my computer, when I was ready to hurl it over the garden hedge, and for their tremendous ongoing support, I thank my daughters Caroline Webb and Janey Volden, and our absolute 'star' family member Jill Veitch for preparing the manuscript and photographs ready for the publisher. To my stepdaughter, Christine Rougier-Chapman and her husband Alwyn, for lending me photographs and for their research into the Hayes' family in Ireland, my love and gratitude. To Charles' son, Michael, and his wife Lynne, for their loving warmth, and the photography they organised for me while staying with them in London, I thank them so much. Ted and Audrey (Charles' cousin) Clarvis, (UK), sent me corrected family background events, for which I am most grateful. An appreciative thanks to Keith Bradley and Mark Wood of the War Museum, Calgary, Canada, for research when I needed it.

For the amusing stories Charles' old friends, Terence Gavaghan (London, UK) and Dr. Ted Margetts, (Vancouver, Canada), told me about him, thank you both for making me smile! And for their encouragement on my completing this book, I am more than grateful to International Sports Commentator, Steve King and his wife Jean -- our first friends in Canada.

All copies of BBC, (The British Broadcasting Corporation), VOK (Voice Of Kenya) broadcasts, most newspaper articles, (with accompanying photographs) used in this book, were written by Charles Hayes and found in his filing cabinet.

Margaret Ann Hayes
Okanagan Falls, British Columbia, Canada
2004

Index

ISBN 141201411-5